TRICOTER

Simply Beautiful
Sweaters

BERYL HIATT AND LINDEN PHELPS

Martingale
& COMPANY

Bothell, Washington

Simply Beautiful Sweaters
© 1999 by Beryl Hiatt and Linden Phelps
Martingale & Company, PO Box 118, Bothell, WA 98041-0118 USA

Printed in Hong Kong
04 03 02 01 00 99   6 5 4 3 2 1

FIBER
STUDIO
PRESS

Fiber Studio Press is an imprint of Martingale & Company.

Library of Congress Cataloging-in-Publication Data
Hiatt, Beryl.
　　　　Simply beautiful sweaters / Beryl Hiatt and Linden Phelps.
　　　　p.　　　cm.
　　　　Includes bibliographical references (p.　).
　　　　ISBN 1-56477-255-1
　　　　1. Knitting—Patterns.　2. Sweaters.　I. Phelps, Linden.
　　II. Title.　III. Title: Simply beautiful sweaters.
　　TT825.H53　1999
　　746.43'20432—dc21　　　　　　　　　　　　　　98-43432
　　　　　　　　　　　　　　　　　　　　　　　　　　　CIP

Credits

President: Nancy J. Martin
CEO/Publisher: Daniel J. Martin
Associate Publisher: Jane Hamada
Editorial Director: Mary V. Green
Design and Production Manager: Cheryl Stevenson
Technical Editing: Ursula Reikes
Editing and Design: Watershed Books
Copy Editing: Liz McGehee
Illustration: Robin Strobel
Photography: Brent Kane

MISSION STATEMENT

WE ARE DEDICATED TO PROVIDING QUALITY PRODUCTS AND SERVICE BY WORKING TOGETHER TO INSPIRE CREATIVITY AND TO ENRICH THE LIVES WE TOUCH.

DEDICATION

This book, our first, is dedicated with love and gratitude, to our mothers.

From Beryl to Beulah

You taught me how to make yarn move between my fingers, igniting a passion for knitting that has shaped my life. You never hesitated to provide the most beautiful and luxurious yarns, even when my stitches were uneven and irregular. You allowed me to spend long hours in yarn shops on Saturdays throughout my childhood, and you have shared my joy in the successes of my work, all the while admonishing me not to work too hard, grow too fast, or take on too much. For your love and concern, support and pride, I dedicate this to you, Mom.

From Lindy to Ruth

I have always admired the incredible beauty of your music, envied the fact that you came to your passion so early in life, and remember how it seemed to envelop us all in one way or another, growing up. I remember begging you not to sing those "funny Italian songs" when our friends came to visit and mimicking your students as they practiced their scales. I also remember the pride and excitement of being included in "adult dinners" after your performances.

After a number of years pursuing several "careers," I finally understood your passion for music when I discovered mine for hand knitting! I realized how it can "take over one's life." I never leave the house without my knitting (who knows what delays may occur throughout the day that allow me a few minutes to knit!). I've carried it with me to dinner parties, basketball games, and concerts, and I have come to understand that the true enjoyment is in the process of knitting—sometimes even more than the pleasure of the completed sweater.

This book is dedicated with love to you, Mom, for showing me by your own example the importance of finding and following my personal passion. Thank you for your unconditional love and support.

ACKNOWLEDGMENTS

The Tricoter Staff, front row (left to right): Rose, Stacy, Yiming, Elizabeth; back row (left to right): Tanya, Ola, Beryl, Lindy, Julie, Ingrid, Dinny

Staff

◆ First and foremost, Ingrid, without whom this book could not have happened—her incredible eye for color, design, and detail inspires us daily;

◆ Rose, whose vast knowledge is surpassed only by her patience and grace;

◆ Dinny, our rock, who has taught us that we can do it all ourselves;

◆ Stacy, for details that make sweaters beautiful enough to wear inside out;

◆ Tanya, whose unbridled joy, enthusiasm, and passion reinspire us constantly;

◆ Ola, our magician, who performs daily miracles with sweaters;

◆ Yiming, the ultimate technician and the most beautiful knitter in the world;

◆ Julie, a creative treasure we would love to clone;

◆ Elizabeth, a seamstress and knitter with a wonderful eye for color and texture; and

◆ Eva, who has retired but will remain always in our hearts

Extended "Staff"

◆ Monica, cheerleader, teacher, designer, and probably the best customer any store could dream of;

◆ Sue Hovis, whose passion for knitting and desire to pass it on to the next generation of knitters is her raison d'être; and

◆ Dr. Sam, who proved that knitting is not just a woman's domain . . . and who brought us a new perspective on design.

Extended Family

◆ Elisabetta, our "sister," who dares to dream dreams with us, and whose beauty, strength, and integrity challenge us never to accept less from ourselves; and

◆ Stacy, our "brother," mentor, friend, and confidant. His encouragement, support, and commitment to us and to the hand-knitting industry are unmatched!

Our Sisters

◆ Leslie, for your unconditional love and support; you really are "the wind beneath my wings;" and

◆ Vernette, who convinced me to follow my dreams and challenged me not to take the easy road.

Our Editor

◆ A very special thank you to Ursula Reikes, technical editor, artist, perfectionist, and dear friend, who taught us the true meaning of detail and consistency.

Contents

THE STORY OF TRICOTER   7
    Our Philosophy of Knitting   8

GETTING STARTED   13
    Finding Your Inspiration   13
    The Knitter's Necessities   13
    A Second Project   15

KNITTING SWEATERS THAT FIT!   17
    Determining the Right
      Dimensions for You   17
    Knitting Your Swatch   17
    Determining Your Gauge   18
    Checking Your Gauge   19

HOW TO READ A TRICOTER PATTERN   21
    Knitting Terms and Abbreviations   23

TWENTY PATTERNS FOR
    BEAUTIFULLY SIMPLE SWEATERS   25

    FABULOUS FIRST PROJECTS
      Crewneck Pullover   26
      Cowlneck Pullover   31

    QUICK CROPPED PULLOVERS
      Seed Stitch Pullover   36
      Easy Basic Pullover   41

    READY FOR RIBBING
      Ribbed Jacket   46
      Ribbed Pullover   53

    EASY, BREEZY TOPS
      Cropped Cardigan   58
      Striped Pullover   62

    SIMPLE SUMMER SHAPES
      Sleeveless Cardigan   66
      Back Button Top   71

    TERRIFIC TEES
      Striped Tee-Shirt   76
      Ribbon Tee-Shirt   80

SUPER SUMMER CARDIGANS
    Ribbed Fitted Cardigan   84
    Ribbed Striped Cardigan   90

ALL-TIME FAVORITE JACKET
    Garter Stitch Jacket   96

CLASSIC CARDIGANS
    Traditional Summer Cardigan   102
    Striped Cardigan   108

SPECTACULAR STRIPING
    Multi-Stripe Pullover   114
    Multi-Stripe Cardigan   120

COLLECTIBLE CABLE
    Short Cabled Pullover   126

SOME KNITTING BASICS   133
    Casting On   133
    Knitting Your Edge Stitches   133
    Picking Up Dropped Stitches   133
    Joining Yarns   134
    Weaving in Ends As You Knit   134
    Increasing Your Stitches   134
    Decreasing Your Stitches   135
    Knitting Basic Cables   135
    Binding Off   135

FINISHING   137
    Sewing Shoulder Seams   137
    Sewing Side Seams   137
    Picking Up Stitches to Knit Bands   137
    Setting in Sleeve Caps   138
    Buttonholes   139
    Crocheted Edges   140
    Stabilizing Back Neck and Shoulders   140
    Blocking   141

RESOURCES   142
    Tricoter Services   142
    Yarn Resources   143

BIBLIOGRAPHY   143

The Story of Tricoter

"When we discover something magical, the joy is in sharing it."

SHEILA LUKINS AND JULEE ROSSO

TRICOTER (Tri'•ko•tay), the French verb meaning "to knit," feels, in retrospect, to be the inevitable destiny of partners Beryl Hiatt and Lindy Phelps. The store, located in Seattle, Washington, is a tribute to the wisdom of true friends who can sometimes see us more clearly than we can see ourselves; the timing of events that bring together the most unlikely individuals; and the electricity of shared passions born of an appreciation for beauty, color, and texture. It speaks also to the ability of the timeless process of knitting to transform the lives of those who succumb to its rhythmic progression of stitches. We believe that we are products of our passions.

Tricoter's success has been due, in great part, to our commitment to help our customers make beautiful sweaters that really fit, to design easy-to-follow patterns that reflect the individual style of each customer, and to provide a broad selection of the most beautiful, luxurious, and colorful fibers available. We are constantly knitting new sample sweaters for inspiration. We provide complete finishing services and can assemble the sweater that has been sitting unfinished in a closet for months, creating guilt, or we can handle the tricky technical parts of completing a sweater that, when properly executed, makes it look truly professional. We also design and custom knit for many clients who love sweaters, but who do not knit themselves.

Tricoter has been described as an "experience" rather than a store by more than one customer. Some have even accused us of being a front for a healing center! Our love of beauty, color, and design was the catalyst for developing a bright, colorful environment (not unlike our living room). But it is the sense of community found within it that makes Tricoter so different from most yarn shops. This sense of community is created, in part, by the large round tables where customers are invited to come and work through challenging details of their projects with expert assistance always close at hand. It is due even more to the unique bond that knitting creates among souls with little else in common. Here friendships are forged by the shared joys and trials inevitably discussed around the tables as women (and a growing number of men) knit.

First opened in the summer of 1984, Tricoter is the result of Beryl's lifelong passion for knitting and her desire to share that passion. A close friend first voiced the obvious: "You have been visiting yarn shops in every city you visit for years, seeking out beautiful fibers and looking for people who share your passion—what more logical direction for you than your own store?" Realizing that this was, indeed, her "destiny" and undaunted by her lack of any formal retail experience, Beryl opened the doors of Tricoter within months! (When asked by a financial analyst what made her think she could be successful with so little retail experience, Beryl's response was "Because I love to entertain and I'm a great hostess." While it drew great laughs, this has truly been an important factor in Tricoter's success.)

Tricoter developed an almost immediate clientele of loyal, creative, passionate knitters who were hungry for the incredible selection of beautiful fibers that lined the walls of the store, and for the help to create sweaters that fit properly. We often have people (some of whom don't knit) stop in just for a "color fix" or general inspiration. There is something about the overwhelming colors and textures of the four walls of the shop—the cubbyholes exploding with yarns and our wall of exotic buttons.

Beryl's own insatiable enthusiasm and the beauty and selection of yarns in the store proved to be a draw for our staff as well. Some of the most talented knitters and finishers in the area, most of whom joined the store within the first year or so, are still at Tricoter today.

Since knitting is a much more integral part of most European cultures than our own, many of the staff provide a distinctly international flavor to the store: Ingrid is from Germany's Black Forest region, Rose is Hungarian-born, Aleksandra is from Poland, Yiming came to us from Bejing, and Beryl is a Canadian citizen. Stacy left the chorus lines of Las Vegas revues to join the Tricoter "team," but that is exotic rather than international!

In 1990, Beryl made the decision to relocate to Madison Park, a small residential neighborhood east of downtown Seattle, much more convenient to most of Tricoter's existing customers—and for many more who had not yet realized their passion for knitting!

As fate would have it, Tricoter opened its doors next to Beans, a brand-new coffee store owned by Lindy Phelps. Beryl and Lindy formed an instant friendship. Beryl stopped by several times a day for lattes, and Lindy frequently dropped in after hours at Tricoter to design the windows and interior displays. Some call it destiny, others luck, but within months, Beryl and Lindy decided to join forces and form a partnership. Beryl's unique sense of style and love of fibers and Lindy's background in store design and merchandising (twelve years heading Visual Merchandising Divisions for May Company department stores and Liz Claiborne, Inc.), along with a combined passion for entertaining, beauty, color, and texture, proved to be a successful combination.

Tricoter has become a place where color, texture, and friendship are stitched together to create the stuff of life.

Our Philosophy of Knitting

Where, when, or more important, why knit? For us, the answers to the first two questions are anytime, anywhere. As for the third, there are times in all of our lives when knitting has helped us through the most challenging situations. And certain types of knitting are more appropriate than others, based on our ability or need to concentrate on, cope with, resolve, or escape a particular situation.

"I don't have time to knit" is no excuse, because some of the most prolific knitters we know are living the most intense, stressful, and busy lives imaginable. We were interviewed in 1997 for an article in *Forbes* magazine on the resurgence of arts and crafts in America. The interviewing editor asked skeptically, "If these are such young, busy, motivated women with full-time careers, children, etc., what are they doing knitting?" The answer is that these women knit precisely because their lives are so intense and challenging. Such highly creative and motivated individuals cannot make the transition from the hectic pace of their day to sleep without a relaxing, yet productive activity.

Knitting can be picked up and put down at any moment without losing your place (unlike reading). Also, it doesn't exclude conversation or socializing. We know many women who actually took up knitting to have something to do while spending weekends with husbands or boyfriends who watch sports, or who knit during their children's Little League games, ballet classes, or gymnastics meets. And

A typical day at Tricoter

knitting allows you to retain full awareness of the beauty that surrounds you in nature. Nothing is more peaceful and spiritually restoring than sitting in a beautiful outdoor setting with your knitting, absorbing the incredible natural beauty, inhaling the clean, fresh air, and just enjoying the moment.

Because we have so few limitations in our own lives as to where and when we knit, we decided to poll our customers to find out where and when they knit. Here are a few of the responses.

◆ On a cruise. "Other passengers wanted to check the progress of my sweater daily, and some even offered

several times the value of the yarn for the finished garment, or wanted the yarn to knit it themselves."

◆ At a Knitter's Book Club meeting. "Members listen to the audio version of a book while they're knitting, then we get together to knit and discuss the book."

◆ After cancer surgery. "Knitting helped me get through my cancer surgery. The simple, repetitive process of knitting was a grounding, calming, and therapeutic process that required minimal concentration while keeping my muscles limber."

◆ On planes, trains, etc. We know knitters who look forward to long flights to Hong Kong, New York, or the

Caribbean, or train trips across entire continents, because they provide uninterrupted knitting time.

♦ In airports when flights are delayed. We know many flight attendants who wouldn't think of getting on a plane without their knitting, and who knit on breaks between serving meals in flight and in lonely hotel rooms on long layovers in strange cities.

♦ During meditation. "It allows me to keep my hands busy and productive, and provides the grounding to relax and free my mind."

♦ When a big decision must be made. "I like to get out of town, find a beautiful, quiet spot—a bench overlooking the ocean; a warm, flat rock on a spot with an endless view of the mountains; or a small, still pond in a beautiful garden—where I can knit and think."

♦ In a Paris sidewalk café. "It's a beautiful way to absorb the people, the beauty, the smells, and the sounds while drinking café au lait with a friend."

♦ When angry. "I knit when I'm angry because it forces me to take time out and reflect on my anger—before I do something I may later regret. I also can't stay angry long when I'm doing something that gives me so much joy."

♦ When anxious. "Knitting is way cheaper than therapy, and I get to wear my work."

♦ Finally, when time is of the essence. We have arranged for overnight delivery and even special couriers to get yarn to customers who couldn't imagine getting on a four- or five-hour flight without enough knitting to keep them going. Many times, the delivery costs as much or more than the yarn!

One of the Tricoter "walls of color"

The extensive collection of Tricoter sample sweaters. Customers often browse through these for design inspiration.

Getting Started

It is important to understand that to make beautiful sweaters you do *not* need to be an artist—knitting will transform you into an artist. It is not necessary to be able to draw or write about what you want to create. You need only imagine the possibilities and discover which colors and textures inspire you, which shapes make you feel good about yourself. Knitting incorporates these three basic concepts—color, texture, and design—which are part of each of our lives.

Finding Your Inspiration

Fall in love with several yarns that appeal to you visually, then sit down and start to get in touch with the yarn by knitting swatches. What yarns do you love to work with? What feels good slipping through your fingers? What needle size makes the yarn look and feel great? What needle size feels good in your hand? What colors and textures come to life when you knit them? The old saying "Never judge a book by its cover" holds true for yarns. Many fibers look very different knitted than they do rolled in a ball.

Many times, the desire to knit a sweater comes from a picture you see. We are constantly ripping pages out of catalogs when we see shapes or color combinations that appeal to us. Occasionally, a border on a rug or needlepoint canvas triggers the design of a great sweater border. Start a notebook and file all your inspirations in it; it makes a great knitter's reference.

We often design patterns for customers using measurements from a favorite sweatshirt or an old, worn-out sweater—a shape they love and feel great in every time they put it on. If the shape works, why not repeat it?

Great buttons are another source of inspiration for us. We're fortunate to have an entire wall of incredible buttons from around the world. The next time you run across those five or six Bakelite buttons in an antique or junk store, buy them—they'll be your starting point for a one-of-a-kind sweater.

The bottom line is that there isn't one "right" place to start. Let your intuition and passion guide you!

The Knitter's Necessities

Getting your knitting supplies in order is like stocking your pantry: when a big storm hits, there is nothing more satisfying than knowing you have all the ingredients you need for that great stew; rich, chocolatey brownies; or your favorite bread-machine recipe. Preparing your knitting bag(s), making sure that you have all the necessary tools for your project, is much the same.

First and foremost (and we can't stress this enough) is a good knitting light! With the proper light, you will avoid damaging your eyes and will enjoy knitting more. We recommend an adjustable high-intensity, low-voltage lamp. You will find that you spend a lot less time ripping out rows of knitting that looked fine to you when knitting in poor light but reveal glaring errors in daylight.

The following is our list of knitting essentials:

◆ A complete set of knitting needles (and a backup pair in the size you are using for your current project). It would be great to be able to start with a pair in each size, but if that isn't possible, purchase a good needle kit and add to it with each project you knit. Many have slots for both circular and straight needles; these are the most useful.

A word here about needles in general. Several types are readily available in knitting stores around the country. In most cases, there isn't one right type; it is just what feels most comfortable to you. Both of us prefer to work on

Just a sampling of our beautiful buttons

straight bamboo needles. We like the feel of the smooth wood and the way the yarn glides evenly against them. Some of our customers wouldn't knit on anything other than metal "turbos," preferring the speed they claim turbos allow them. And still others like the feel of bamboo but prefer circular to straight needles.

In certain cases, the yarn or the design of a project will dictate the type of needle, but in most cases, it is a matter of personal preference. Throws with 100-plus stitches, usually in big, bulky combinations of yarns, would be impossible to fit on straight needles, and many of our customers use circular needles when they travel because they take up less room and won't inadvertently "attack" an unwitting seat mate, etc.

◆ Tape measure. A soft, tailor's tape measure (one that shows inches on one side and centimeters on the other) is most useful, since many patterns are translated from European languages where centimeters are the standard unit of measure. A ruler or hard metal tape measure won't give you an accurate measurement over your soft fabric.

◆ Sharp scissors. We love small needlework scissors that can be worn on a cord around your neck so they are always there when you need them. We recently found wonderful scissors that sit in their own enameled case on a chain. They look like real jewelry and are a great accessory.

◆ Row counters. Some types slip around your needle, and others are like supermarket "clickers"; either version will work.

◆ Several sizes of stitch holders

◆ Cable needles

◆ A good comprehensive reference book (see page 143 for options)

◆ Calculator (critical in determining your gauge)

◆ Stitch markers. The split-ring type is the most versatile.

◆ Point protectors in at least two sizes

◆ Pen and notepad. When you make a change in your pattern, you must write it down; it's amazing what you will forget between one sleeve and the next! Between one row and the next!

◆ Bodkins. These are the large tapestry needles used to sew your sweater together.

◆ Crochet hooks in several sizes. These are invaluable for picking up dropped stitches.

◆ Safety pins. They're great for holding a dropped stitch or marking the last increase made.

◆ Long, stainless-steel T-pins

◆ Needle gauge. When there is no size marked on a needle, it is virtually impossible to determine the exact size.

◆ Nail file or emery board. Use this to get rid of rough nails that snag the yarn as you knit.

◆ A great accessory bag to keep all of your tools together. One that zips is safest; many prefer the ones with smaller sections for organizing your tools.

◆ A pair of magnifier-type reading glasses. Unless your eyes are perfect, these are critical for closeup work.

◆ Zipper-lock bags. When running multiple strands of yarn together as one or when working with skeins that are very slippery and tend to unwind easily, it is helpful to seal the skein(s) in a zipper-lock bag and cut off one corner of the bag to run the strands through. This will save many hours of untangling.

Then there is the next tier, the list of options that aren't essential but make a knitter's life easier:

◆ A ball winder. It makes quick work of changing those big hanks into manageable balls.

◆ A steam table. This wooden table, which is covered in several layers of foam, cotton batting, and fabric, and usually has a grid pattern, is used for blocking your completed garments.

◆ A steamer. It's not only great for steaming sweaters, but we bet you'll find it virtually replaces your iron for most tasks!

◆ More knitting bags. We've found that you need one for each project.

There are many more optional tools, and we're always finding new ones, but this will give you a great setup and meet most of your needs.

A Second Project

There are several reasons to have more than one knitting project going at a time. You may get stuck (run into a snag or make a mistake that you need help to fix). You might run out of yarn or lose a critical skein or needle! You may get bored with or tired of working on one project and need a break from it. Some projects are more challenging and require lots of concentration. These are great when you're all by yourself and thinking clearly, but sometimes you need a "no-brainer": a simple project that is straightforward, easy to knit, and can be worked on while you talk with friends, watch a game, or are exhausted at the end of a long day but want the relaxation that knitting provides.

It is important to note that a no-brainer is not a less exciting sweater by any means; it is just less complicated. Many of our customers tell us it is the no-brainers that they enjoy knitting the most, that they can turn out two or three of these sweaters to one complex sweater—there is a great sense of satisfaction in completion.

The important thing is to always have your knitting—whatever project it is—with you. We can't tell you how many times we've heard, "If I'd only had my knitting, I wouldn't have minded the traffic jam, delayed flight, etc."

Tricoter's collection of Noro Japanese yarns

Knitting
Sweaters that FIT!

Determining the Right Dimensions for You

Who among us is not guilty of purchasing a piece of clothing with the misguided (and ultimately depressing) notion that it will make us look just like the six-foot-two-inch, 105-pound model wearing it in a photograph? The key to great sweater design is to select a silhouette that appeals to you and then adapt the dimensions to fit your body.

Current fashion certainly influences our decisions—sleeves may be narrower one season and wider the next; clothing hugs the body one season, then exaggerated shoulders and looser silhouettes line the runways the next. Despite fashion's fluctuations, the basic dimensions that work best for us individually usually don't vary more than an inch or so. We have found that there are three, or at most four, basic silhouettes that are tried-and-true starting points for our personal sweater designs: longer sweaters worn over leggings or a slim pant; mid-length sweaters that look great with skirts or dresses; and shorter, more fitted sweaters that work for little summer shells or tailored vests.

It is important, too, to remember that you want to look your best in a sweater that you take the time to knit—and don't confuse looking your best with trying to mirror what looks great on someone else. A great friend and customer of ours admitted that when she first came to Tricoter, she would copy many of the sweaters that Beryl had knit for herself—sweaters with intense colors, lots of texture, and usually at least a "hint" of metallic fiber or some other unexpected accent. Although such sweaters look great on Beryl, this customer found that she was always disappointed when she finished such a sweater because she felt overwhelmed by it when she wore it. It was as if the sweater were wearing her. It took almost two years for her to realize that not only was she very different in physical

scale than Beryl, but she also had very different coloring and was much less flamboyant. She has since knit a number of beautiful sweaters in wonderful, soft colors, scaled down in size—sweaters she frequently wears and loves. We learned from this experience that designing sweaters is all about personal style, about designing for *your* lifestyle.

You will note as you read through the patterns in this book that we have specified certain yarns for each sweater. These are the actual yarns used when the sample sweater was knit. In many cases, by the time this book is published, those particular yarns may have been discontinued. We included them to give a frame of reference, but we believe that it is the shape and design of the sweater that is important. We have included basic yarn amounts and gauges as a guide; search for your personal favorite designs and create your sweaters in yarns and colors that reflect your unique personality.

Knitting Your Swatch

This is the most creative part of knitting your sweater. We're always surprised to hear customers complain about "taking the time" to knit a swatch. For us, this is the most exciting point: feeling the yarn, finding out what works, learning how certain stitches show off the beauty of a particular yarn while others get lost in the texture or color, deciding what needle size makes the yarn look and feel best, and discovering what colors work—or don't work—next to others.

Combinations that look beautiful together on a tray may have a completely different feel when knit in various combinations. Knitting swatches is your opportunity to play with color. Cast on twenty stitches or so, and don't be afraid to try unusual combinations or add a color that you normally wouldn't consider. A good friend and avid gardener once reminded us that color in sweaters is no different than in a garden. While you would probably never plant a whole garden of marigolds, the accent that they add when combined with the colorful palette of other flowers brings all the colors to life.

The placement of color is just as important as the selection of the overall palette. Beryl noticed this when she was swatching for a summer vest on a plane trip to San Francisco several years ago. She had selected six colors (three solids and three multicolors) of a new yarn that she was crazy about and decided on a color-work pattern that she wanted to use. As we took off, she settled in to knit her swatch, confident that she would be well into the actual knitting of the vest by the time we landed. Two hours and four or five different combinations later, she finally hit upon just the right placement—using the same six colors she had originally started with. One of the lessons we owe to years of studying Missoni color work (unquestionably the modern-day masters of color!) is that colors work best when used in unexpected combinations. Many times, the pattern in color work is lost when colors used next to each other are too close and end up blending into each other.

Your swatch is also your opportunity to explore new ground, to experiment outside your comfort zone. There is very little lost over twenty stitches. It is much less painful than tearing out 8" of painstaking knitting on a sweater when you realize that the total color repeat you selected doesn't look the way you envisioned. Swatching is your opportunity to explore new stitches, to test new techniques. Find out what kinds of stitches you enjoy working with and which ones are too confusing or difficult to execute on the yarn you have chosen. (As a rule, cotton and linen yarns have very little give, whereas wool, cashmere, and many blends are much more pliable or forgiving.) It is important not to force a swatch just to get a gauge (although this is a critical benefit). Remember that when it all comes together, it will look and feel right to you. If this isn't happening after a few tries, add a new yarn or different stitch, or put it

down and look for a different idea altogether. To enjoy the process of knitting, it is important to love your swatch first. If you burn out on the swatch, you can be sure you won't enjoy knitting a whole project based on it.

> If you intend to wash your garment, it is a good idea to wash your swatch (following the manufacturer's directions), particularly when knitting with high-contrast colors or a dark or bright color with white. This will ensure colorfastness and let you know how the fiber(s) will respond.
>
> TRICOTER
> Knitting specialists

One of the most frustrating comments we hear is "I stopped knitting because nothing I knit ever turned out the way it was supposed to; it never fit!" While knitting is not an exact science, it certainly shouldn't be a random "shot in the dark" either. It is an easy-to-estimate and simple-to-adjust process when approached with some basic tools. Knitting a swatch to determine your gauge is the first critical step.

Determining Your Gauge

Gauge, or tension, is the most important factor in creating sweaters that really fit. All patterns are based on a specific number of stitches and rows per inch. If your knitting does not match those specifications, your garment will not fit properly.

To determine gauge, knit a sample swatch with the yarn and needles you will use for your garment. Always knit a swatch at least 4" wide and 4" long. Because the stitches at the end of each row of knitting tend to be somewhat distorted, measure at least one stitch in from the selvage edges of the swatch. Therefore, cast on at least two more stitches than needed to make 4" of knitting width. Work the specified pattern stitch to check the gauge; if no pattern is given, work the swatch in stockinette stitch. If the pattern is complex (color work or lace), work a larger swatch, perhaps 6" to 8" square.

To measure the swatch, lay it flat. Place a tape measure parallel to a row of stitches and count the number of stitches (including fractions of inches) that make 4". Now divide the number of stitches in the 4" swatch by 4 to get the number of stitches per inch. This is your gauge. Compare this gauge to the one specified in your pattern. If your swatch has too few stitches, your work is too loose; try again with smaller needles. If your swatch has too many stitches, your work is too tight; try larger needles or a different yarn.

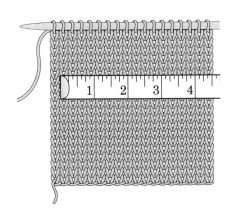

When your gauge matches the one specified by the pattern, you are ready to begin knitting. The gauge swatch may be saved or pulled out and reused. You can bind off the stitches and use the swatch to test the washability and colorfastness of the yarn(s), or save it in a notebook or file with other swatches for future reference.

The next step is to take your gauge (the number of stitches per inch) and multiply that by the number of inches of width you want your finished garment to measure. As you knit, lay your work flat without stretching it; measure every few inches to see if your gauge has changed. When knitting on straight needles, it is important to stop halfway across the row so you can lay your work completely flat to measure it.

Checking Your Gauge

Continue to measure your garment every few inches as you work to ensure that it remains on gauge. This check is particularly important if you set your work down for extended periods of time between knitting. Your tension may vary as your life changes; for example, it may be tighter when you are tense, looser when you are more relaxed. It is also important to measure the length of your work by holding it upright. Let it hang as it would if it were being worn, so you can see the actual length of the garment.

Remember to measure both the length and width of the piece as you knit. To measure an area that has been shaped, such as an armhole or sleeve, measure perpendicular to the bottom edge by laying a straight edge horizontally across the garment, even with the first row of bound-off stitches. From that straight edge, measure vertically to the lower edge of the knitting needle. On a sleeve, measure along the center of the sleeve. Do not follow along the slanted side edge.

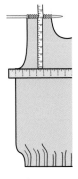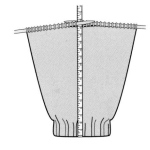

Measuring an armhole   Measuring a sleeve

It is not uncommon for your gauge to change significantly if you become fatigued or unable to concentrate. It is relatively simple to adjust your pattern, increasing or decreasing a couple of stitches at this point to compensate. This is a habit you should get into and continue to practice throughout all of your knitting.

To compensate for a slight variance from the original pattern, the number of stitches on the front of a garment may vary slightly from the back. However, by the time you are ready for neck and shoulder shaping, your front and back *must* match. They should have the same number of stitches and the same shoulder shaping.

How To Read a
Tricoter Pattern

Because we are very visual, we tend to approach life, and more specifically knitting, from a very visual perspective. Often, we find it helpful to sketch a sweater in the design phase, just to help visualize the scale and such specific design elements as the placement of striping or pockets. We devised our pattern forms for this reason. These are the forms that we use in the store when we create a pattern with our customers.

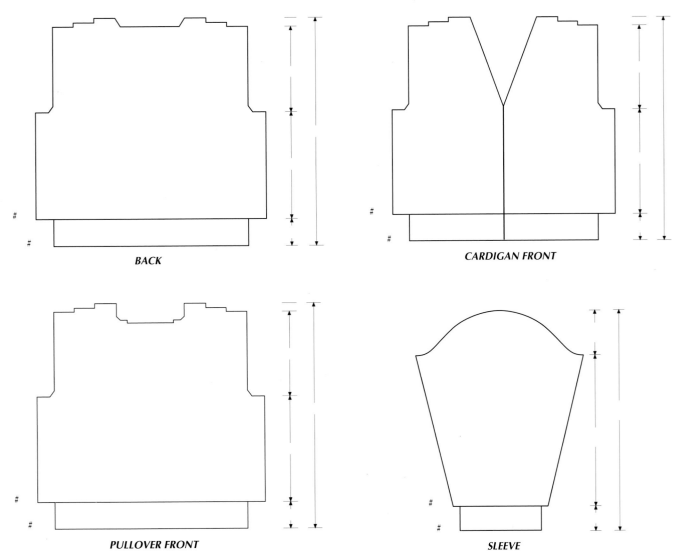

BACK

CARDIGAN FRONT

PULLOVER FRONT

SLEEVE

The forms are designed to reflect the basic shape of the actual piece that you are knitting. The intent is to make it easier for you to relate specific directions to the actual part of the sweater that you are working on.

On our actual store pattern forms, we include a space at the top for a name and telephone number so that you have a better chance of having the pattern returned to you, should you leave it behind or misplace it. We also have places to record your specific gauge, needle sizes, and amount of yarn(s) used. This is an invaluable reference, not only while you are knitting the sweater, but also in the event that you (or someone else) want to knit a similar sweater in the future. Information that is crystal clear in your mind today can often be a blur in a few days.

The measurements for the total length of the garment appear at the far right side of the page; next to them are the incremental measurements for ribbing and lower-body lengths, armhole depth, and shoulder shaping. Throughout the directions you will see a set of numbers in brackets: for example

[72 (80, 86) sts; 20" (22", 24") wide]. This indicates the number of stitches you should have on your needle and how wide your work should be at a particular point in the process.

The pattern itself is intended to be read as a garment is knit: from bottom to top. We write the initial needle sizes, the number of stitches to cast on, and the pattern stitch for the ribbing or bottom of the garment at the bottom of the page. Depending on the space and the complexity of the sweater, we also lay out the "setup" row(s) in this space.

As you read up the sheet, we outline the points at which you should change needle sizes, any increases and/or decreases that are necessary, and pattern or stitch information for the body of the garment. We strongly recommend that you measure your work frequently to ensure proper fit and avoid having to rip out your work. If, after knitting several inches, you find that your sweater is slightly too large or too small, it is not too late to add or decrease a couple of stitches. Make the appropriate notes to remind yourself to make the front(s) slightly wider or

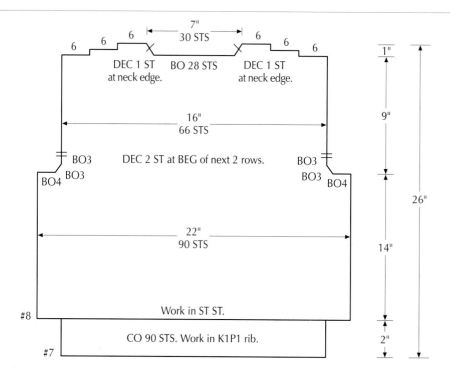

narrower to compensate, or if necessary, recalculate your gauge and begin again. Remember, you can make informed decisions, but in the end, knitting is more art than science.

On patterns that require armhole shaping, we specify the number, type, and frequency of decreases to achieve the desired shaping. On most sweater backs, the back neck shaping and shoulder shaping will happen concurrently. We believe this is critical to ensure the proper fit of a sweater. While this may be a departure for many of you from the way you are used to knitting sweaters, and therefore confusing, we have laid it out as graphically as possible. After making a sweater using this technique, most of our customers find it quite easy to follow. Our written directions walk you through these steps row by row.

In the case of deep V-necks on sweater fronts, it may be necessary to begin neck shaping decreases either slightly sooner or later than the armhole shaping. These notations are clearly specified, and we generally tell you

how many inches from the bottom of your garment you should be when these events occur.

On many sweater fronts, the neck shaping will occur several inches before or almost concurrently with the shoulder shaping. Again, remember to measure frequently to ensure proper length. It is also helpful to use your sweater back as a guide for shaping the front; remember, they need to line up.

Sleeve patterns read basically the same: from bottom to top. Measurements for length are again along the right-hand side of the page. On most of our sweater patterns, we shape the cap of the sleeve. This is the portion of the sleeve that connects to the body of the sweater. Proper cap shaping ensures that the sleeve fits into the armhole as neatly as possible for a better-fitting garment. Sleeves that are designed to fit into armholes with less (or no) armhole shaping on the body of the garment require a smaller or shallower sleeve cap. On sweaters that have deeper armhole shaping (for a closer fit), deeper cap shaping is required.

Knitting Terms and Abbreviations

beg	begin or beginning		K	knit	
bo	bind off		P	purl	
co	cast on		rep	repeat	
cont	continue		rib	ribbing	
dec	decrease	noted by "/" or "\" symbols on edges or at neckline	RS	right side	
EOR	every other row		seed st	seed stitch	knit 1 stitch, purl 1 stitch, offset stitches on next row
garter st or G ST	garter stitch	knit every row (when doing garter st in the round, for example, on necks, knit 1 row, purl 1 row)	st/sts	stitch/stitches	
			St st	stockinette stitch	knit 1 row, purl 1 row
			SL	slip	as if to purl unless otherwise noted
inc	increase	noted by "X" symbol at edges of pattern	WS	wrong side	

20 Patterns for

Beautifully

Simple

Sweaters

Fabulous First Projects

CREWNECK PULLOVER

The hardest part of becoming a knitter is getting started on your first sweater. That's what we keep hearing from our new customers. This pattern is designed to overcome that fear, help you learn to love knitting, and create—in a very short time—a truly beautiful sweater that you will really wear. The pattern is simple: very little shaping, a big gauge and needle size, and most of all, a great shape for almost any body type. We've chosen yarns we are particularly fond of for examples in this book, but the key to creating a sweater you want to wear is to select a yarn that you really love. Just make sure you find one that knits to our gauge, or adjust your needle size to get the required gauge.

Incidentally, this was the very first sweater Lindy ever knit! She fell in love with the wonderful, luxurious mohair and decided to try her hand at knitting. The rest, as they say, is history!

Size

Small (Medium, Large)
Finished Bust: 40" (44", 48")
Finished Length: 26" (28", 30")

Materials

Use a yarn that knits at 3.5 sts to 1".
11 (12, 13) skeins of Filatura di Crosa
  Belcanto, each approximately
  71 yds. [725 (800, 850) yds. total]
#10½ and #10¾ needles
#10½ circular needle (16" or 20")

Gauge

14 sts and 18 rows = 4" in St st using
  #10¾ needles
Always check gauge before starting
  sweater. Increase or decrease
  needle size to obtain correct gauge.

Back

1. With #10½ needles, cast on 72 (80,
   86) sts. Work in K1, P1 rib for 2".
2. Switch to #10¾ needles. Work in
   St st until work measures 25"
   (27", 29") from bottom [20" (22",
   24") wide].

3. Beg back neck and shoulder
   shaping:
   - Bind off first 8 (9, 10) sts. Knit
     next 16 (19, 21) sts. Keeping 17
     (20, 22) sts on right-hand needle,
     bind off center 22 sts. Finish row.
     Turn work.
   - Bind off first 8 (9, 10) sts. Purl
     across row. Turn work.
   - Dec 1 st at neck edge. Finish
     row. Turn work.
   - Bind off 8 (9, 10) sts. Purl across
     row. Turn work.
   - Knit across row. Turn work.
   - Bind off last 8 (10, 11) sts.
4. Complete back neck and shoulder
   shaping:
   - Join yarn at neck edge; dec 1 st
     and purl across row. Turn work.
   - Bind off 8 (9, 10) sts. Finish row.
     Turn work.
   - Purl across row. Turn work.
   - Bind off last 8 (10, 11) sts.

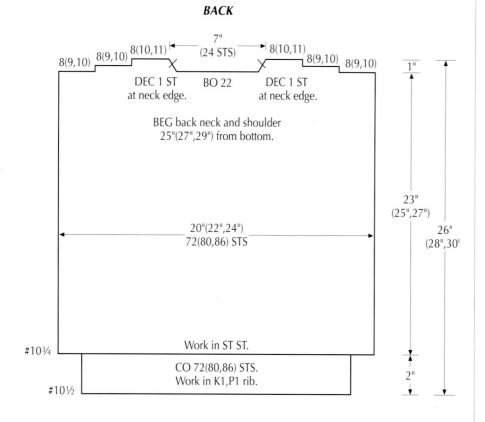

BACK

8(9,10) 8(9,10) 8(10,11) 7" (24 STS) 8(10,11) 8(9,10) 8(9,10)

DEC 1 ST at neck edge.   BO 22   DEC 1 ST at neck edge.

BEG back neck and shoulder 25"(27",29") from bottom.

1"

23" (25",27")

20"(22",24") 72(80,86) STS

26" (28",30')

Work in ST ST.

#10¾

CO 72(80,86) STS. Work in K1,P1 rib.

2"

#10½

Front

1. Work the front exactly the same as the back until work measures 23" (25", 27") from bottom.
2. Beg front neck shaping:
   - ◆ Knit first 30 (34, 37) sts. Bind off center 12 sts. Finish row. Turn work.
   - ◆ Purl across to the neck edge. Turn work.
   - ◆ Bind off first 3 sts at neck edge. Knit across row. Turn work.
   - ◆ Purl across row. Turn work.
   - ◆ Dec 1 st at neck edge EOR 3 times.
3. Cont until work measures 25" (27", 29") from bottom.
4. Beg shoulder shaping:
   - ◆ Bind off first 8 (9, 10) sts. Purl across row. Turn work.
   - ◆ Knit across row. Turn work.
   - ◆ Bind off 8 (9, 10) sts. Purl across row. Turn work.
   - ◆ Knit across row. Turn work.
   - ◆ Bind off last 8 (10, 11) sts.
5. Complete front neck shaping:
   - ◆ Join yarn at neck edge. Bind off first 3 sts. Purl across row. Turn work.
   - ◆ Knit across row. Turn work.
   - ◆ Dec 1 st at neck edge EOR 3 times.
6. Cont until work measures 25" (27", 29") from bottom.
7. Complete shoulder shaping:
   - ◆ Bind off first 8 (9, 10) sts. Knit across row. Turn work.
   - ◆ Purl across row. Turn work.
   - ◆ Bind off 8 (9, 10) sts. Knit across row. Turn work.
   - ◆ Purl across row. Turn work.
   - ◆ Bind off last 8 (10, 11) sts.

FRONT

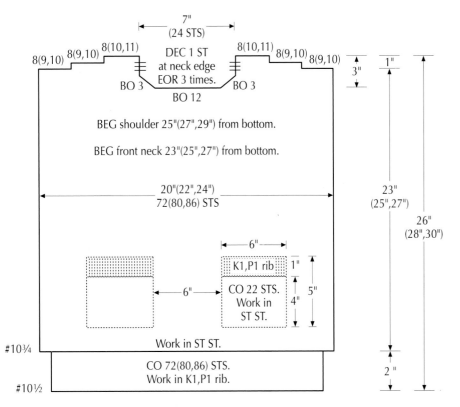

29

Sleeves

1. With #10½ needles, cast on 30 (32, 34) sts. Work in K1, P1 rib for 2".
2. Switch to #10¾ needles. Working in St st, inc 4 sts evenly across first row [34 (36, 38) sts; 9" (10", 11") wide].
3. Cont in St st, inc 1 st at each end every 3 rows 15 (18, 20) times [64 (72, 78) sts; 18" (20", 22") wide].
4. Cont until work measures 15" (16", 17") from bottom.
5. Beg sleeve-cap shaping:
   - Bind off 6 (7, 8) sts at beg of next 6 rows.
   - Bind off 7 (8, 8) sts at beg of next 2 rows.
   - Bind off last 14 sts.

Finishing

1. Sew shoulder seams.
2. Neckband: With RS facing and #10½ circular needle, pick up a total of 68 sts:
   - 28 sts from shoulder to shoulder across back neck
   - 40 sts from shoulder to shoulder across front neck
   - Work in K1, P1 rib for 1½". Bind off loosely in pattern.
3. Make 2 pockets:
   - With #10½ needles, cast on 22 sts.
   - Work in St st for 4".
   - Work 1" more in K1, P1 rib. Bind off in pattern.
4. Place bottom of pocket 1" above ribbing and slipstitch in place.
5. Sew in sleeve caps; sew side and sleeve seams.
6. Block assembled sweater to desired measurements.
7. Stabilize back neck and shoulders.

SLEEVE

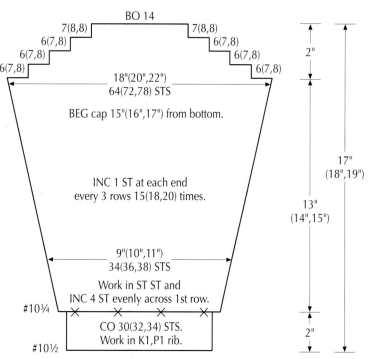

BO 14

7(8,8)   7(8,8)
6(7,8)   6(7,8)
6(7,8)   6(7,8)
6(7,8)   6(7,8)

18"(20",22")
64(72,78) STS

BEG cap 15"(16",17") from bottom.

INC 1 ST at each end
every 3 rows 15(18,20) times.

2"

17"
(18",19")

13"
(14",15")

9"(10",11")
34(36,38) STS

Work in ST ST and
INC 4 ST evenly across 1st row.

#10¾

CO 30(32,34) STS.
Work in K1,P1 rib.

#10½

2"

COWLNECK PULLOVER

We knit all the time to make sure we have plenty of current samples in our store, but we keep coming back to the same dimensions, and frequently to the same shapes, when designing new sweaters. This is due not to a lack of creativity, but rather to the reality that we tend to look good and therefore feel good in those particular silhouettes and dimensions. (Most experienced knitters have three or four favorite silhouettes and dimensions that they keep coming back to.)

It is the beauty of the yarn more than any other factor that makes a sweater special. We may add a pattern stitch or cable, change the neck, or add cuffs to the sleeves, but the basic shape and size remain the same. In this version we added cuffs to the sleeves and simple armhole shaping to minimize the bulk under the arms. To give it an entirely different look, we added a cowl neck and eliminated the pockets.

Size

Small (Medium, Large)

Finished Bust: 40" (44", 48")

Finished Length: 26¹/₂" (27¹/₂", 28¹/₂")

Materials

Use a yarn that knits at 3.0 sts to 1".

12 (13, 14) skeins of Filatura di Crosa
 Ariete, each approximately 55 yds.
 [660 (715, 770) yds. total]

#10 needles

#10 circular needle (16" or 20")

Gauge

12 sts and 15 rows = 4" in St st
 using #10 needles

Always check gauge before starting
 sweater. Increase or decrease
 needle size to obtain correct gauge.

Back

1. With #10 needles, cast on 62
 (68, 74) sts. Work in St st until
 work measures 16¹/₂" (17",
 17¹/₂") from bottom [20"
 (22", 24") wide].

2. Beg armhole shaping:
 ◆ Bind off 3 (5, 7) sts at beg of
 next 2 rows [56 (58, 60) sts;
 18" (19", 20") wide].

3. Cont until work measures 25¹/₂"
 (26¹/₂", 27¹/₂") from bottom.

4. Beg back neck and shoulder
 shaping:
 ◆ Bind off first 6 sts. Knit next 12
 (13, 14) sts. Keeping 13
 (14, 15) sts on right-hand needle,
 bind off center 18 sts and finish
 row. Turn work.

◆ Bind off first 6 sts. Purl across
 row. Turn work.
◆ Dec 1 st at neck edge. Knit
 across row. Turn work.
◆ Bind off 6 (6, 7) sts. Purl across
 row. Turn work.
◆ Knit across row. Turn work.
◆ Bind off last 6 (7, 7) sts.

5. Complete back neck and shoulder
 shaping:
 ◆ Join yarn at neck edge. Dec 1 st
 and finish row. Turn work.
 ◆ Bind off 6 (6, 7) sts. Knit across
 row. Turn work.
 ◆ Purl across row. Turn work.
 ◆ Bind off last 6 (7, 7) sts.

When knitting with a heavily textured yarn, where there is little visible difference between the knit and purl sides of the work, place a large safety pin on the knit side of your work. This will remind you that when the pin is facing you, you are on a knit row; when it is on the back of the work, you are on a purl row.

TRICOTER
Knitting specialists

BACK

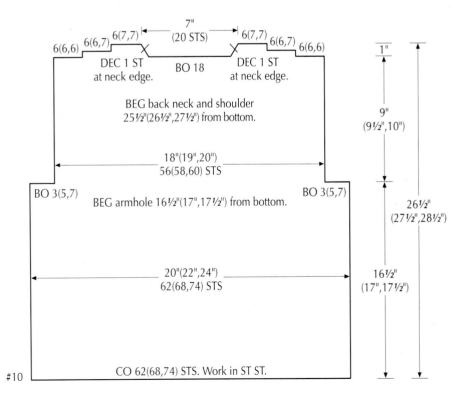

7"
(20 STS)

6(6,6) 6(6,7) 6(7,7)   6(7,7) 6(6,7) 6(6,6)

DEC 1 ST
at neck edge.   BO 18   DEC 1 ST
 at neck edge.

BEG back neck and shoulder
25¹/₂"(26¹/₂",27¹/₂") from bottom.

18"(19",20")
56(58,60) STS

BO 3(5,7)   BO 3(5,7)
BEG armhole 16¹/₂"(17",17¹/₂") from bottom.

20"(22",24")
62(68,74) STS

#10   CO 62(68,74) STS. Work in ST ST.

1"

9"
(9¹/₂",10")

26¹/₂"
(27¹/₂",28¹/₂")

16¹/₂"
(17",17¹/₂")

Front

1. Work the front exactly the same as the back until work measures 23$\frac{1}{2}$" (24$\frac{1}{2}$", 25$\frac{1}{2}$") from bottom.

2. Beg front neck and shoulder shaping:
   - Knit first 24 (25, 26) sts. Bind off center 8 sts. Finish row. Turn work.
   - Purl across row. Turn work.
   - Bind off 3 sts at neck edge. Knit across row. Turn work.
   - Purl across row. Turn work.
   - Dec 1 st at neck edge EOR 3 times.
   - Bind off first 6 sts. Purl across row. Turn work.
   - Knit across row. Turn work.
   - Bind off 6 (6, 7) sts. Purl across row. Turn work.
   - Knit across row. Turn work.
   - Bind off last 6 (7, 7) sts.

3. Complete front neck and shoulder shaping:
   - Join yarn at neck edge. Bind off 3 sts. Purl across row. Turn work.
   - Knit across row. Turn work.
   - Dec 1 st at neck edge EOR 3 times.
   - Bind off first 6 sts. Knit across row. Turn work.
   - Purl across row. Turn work.
   - Bind off 6 (6, 7) sts. Knit across row. Turn work.
   - Purl across row. Turn work.
   - Bind off last 6 (7, 7) sts.

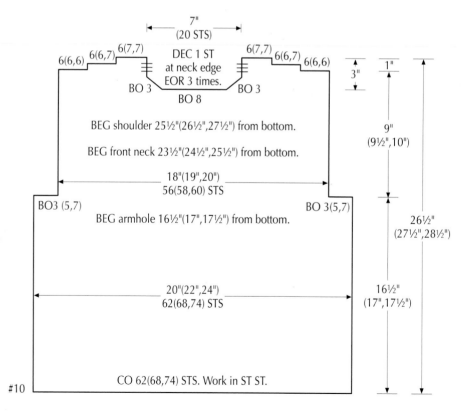

FRONT

7"
(20 STS)

6(6,6) 6(6,7) 6(7,7)   DEC 1 ST at neck edge EOR 3 times.   6(7,7) 6(6,7) 6(6,6)

BO 3   BO 8   BO 3

3"   1"

BEG shoulder 25$\frac{1}{2}$"(26$\frac{1}{2}$",27$\frac{1}{2}$") from bottom.

BEG front neck 23$\frac{1}{2}$"(24$\frac{1}{2}$",25$\frac{1}{2}$") from bottom.

9"
(9$\frac{1}{2}$",10")

18"(19",20")
56(58,60) STS

BO3 (5,7)   BO 3(5,7)

BEG armhole 16$\frac{1}{2}$"(17",17$\frac{1}{2}$") from bottom.

26$\frac{1}{2}$"
(27$\frac{1}{2}$",28$\frac{1}{2}$")

20"(22",24")
62(68,74) STS

16$\frac{1}{2}$"
(17",17$\frac{1}{2}$")

CO 62(68,74) STS. Work in ST ST.

#10

Sleeves

1. With #10 needles, cast on 26 (30, 34) sts. Work in St st for 6" [9" (10", 11") wide]. This is the cuff, 3" of which will be folded back on itself.
2. Work 1" more in St st.
3. Beg sleeve increase:
   - Inc 1 st at each end every 3 rows 12 times [50 (54, 58) sts; 17" (18", 19") wide].
4. Cont until work measures 20" (21", 22") from bottom.

5. Beg sleeve-cap shaping:
   - Bind off 4 sts at beg of next 2 rows.
   - Bind off 4 (4, 5) sts at beg of next 2 rows.
   - Bind off 4 (5, 5) sts at beg of next 6 rows.
   - Bind off last 10 sts.

Finishing

1. Sew shoulder seams.
2. Cowlneck: With RS facing and #10 circular needle, pick up a total of 68 sts:
   - 26 sts from shoulder to shoulder across back neck
   - 42 sts from shoulder to shoulder across front neck
   - Work in St st for 6". Bind off loosely.
3. Sew in sleeve caps; sew side and sleeve seams.
4. Fold back 3" of each sleeve cuff and stitch in place.
5. Block assembled sweater to desired measurements.
6. Stabilize back neck and shoulders.

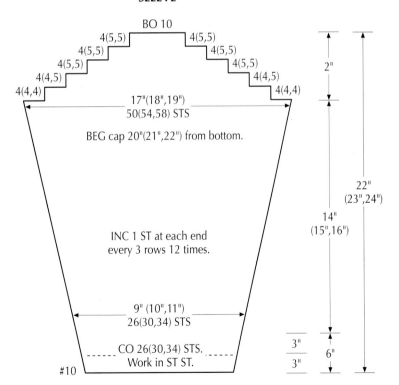

SLEEVE

BO 10

4(5,5)   4(5,5)
4(5,5)   4(5,5)
4(5,5)   4(5,5)
4(4,5)   4(4,5)
4(4,4)   4(4,4)

17"(18",19")
50(54,58) STS

BEG cap 20"(21",22") from bottom.

2"

22"
(23",24")

14"
(15",16")

INC 1 ST at each end
every 3 rows 12 times.

9" (10",11")
26(30,34) STS

CO 26(30,34) STS.
Work in ST ST.

3"
3"

6"

#10

Quick Cropped Pullovers

SEED STITCH PULLOVER

This is another favorite sweater with beginners that is just as popular with experienced knitters, who love the simple, yet sophisticated look. It is the perfect "mindless" knitting project to take with you on a car trip or vacation because it is simple enough that it doesn't require all your concentration. We sometimes call these "conversational" projects because you can knit and carry on a conversation at the same time without losing your place. We don't, however, suggest cocktail-hour knitting as a rule. We've found (from personal experience) that some of the oddest things occur with just half a glass of wine. We often have spent more time taking out a section with a mistake than we did knitting it originally the evening before!

The key to the success of this sweater is in finding a yarn that you love and that feels great against your skin. This is one sweater you will wear out before you tire of wearing it!

Size

Small (Medium, Large)
Finished Bust: 38" (40", 42")
Finished Length: 18" (19", 20")

Materials

Use a yarn that knits at 3.0 sts to 1".
11 (12, 13) skeins of Schachenmayr
  Lusso, each approximately 61 yds.
  [660 (720, 780) yds. total]
#8 and #9 needles
#8 circular needle (24")

Gauge

12 sts and 21 rows = 4" in seed st
  using #9 needles
Always check gauge before starting
  sweater. Increase or decrease
  needle size to obtain correct gauge.

Seed Stitch

Even number of stitches:
Row 1 (RS): *K1, P1, rep from
  * to end.
Row 2 (WS): *P1, K1, rep from
  * to end.
Repeat rows 1 and 2.

Back

1. With #9 needles, cast on 54
   (58, 62) sts. Switch immediately to
   #8 needles. Work in seed st for 1".
2. Switch to #9 needles and cont in
   seed st; inc 1 st at each end every
   3" 2 times [58 (62, 66) sts; 19"
   (20", 21") wide].
3. Cont until work measures 17"
   (18", 19") from bottom.
4. Beg back neck and shoulder
   shaping:
   ♦ Bind off first 6 (7, 7) sts. Work
     next 13 (14, 16) sts. Keeping 14
     (15, 17) sts on right-hand needle,
     bind off center 18 sts. Finish row.
     Turn work.
   ♦ Bind off first 6 (7, 7) sts. Finish
     row. Turn work.
   ♦ Dec 1 st at neck edge. Finish
     row. Turn work.
   ♦ Bind off 6 (7, 8) sts. Finish row.
     Turn work.
   ♦ Work across row. Turn work.
   ♦ Bind off last 7 (7, 8) sts.
5. Complete back neck and shoulder
   shaping:
   ♦ Join yarn at neck edge. Dec 1 st
     and finish row. Turn work.
   ♦ Bind off 6 (7, 8) sts. Finish row.
     Turn work.
   ♦ Work across row. Turn work.
   ♦ Bind off last 7 (7, 8) sts.

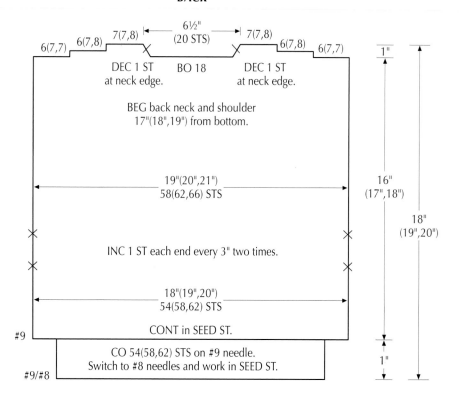

BACK

Front

1. Work the front exactly the same as the back until work measures 15½" (16½", 17½") from bottom.

2. Beg front neck shaping:
   - Work first 24 (26, 28) sts. Keeping 25 (27, 29) sts on right-hand needle, bind off center 10 sts. Finish row. Turn work.
   - Work across row. Turn work.
   - Bind off first 3 sts at neck edge. Finish row. Turn work.
   - Work across row. Turn work.
   - Dec 1 st at neck edge EOR 2 times.

3. Cont until work measures 17" (18", 19") from bottom.

4. Beg shoulder shaping:
   - Beg at outside edge, bind off first 6 (7, 7) sts. Finish row. Turn work.
   - Work across row. Turn work.
   - Bind off 6 (7, 8) sts. Finish row. Turn work.
   - Work across row. Turn work.
   - Bind off last 7 (7, 8) sts.

5. Complete front neck shaping:
   - Join yarn at neck edge. Bind off first 3 sts. Finish row. Turn work.
   - Work across row. Turn work.

   - Dec 1 st at neck edge EOR 2 times.

6. Cont until work measures 17" (18", 19") from bottom.

7. Complete shoulder shaping:
   - Beg at outside edge, bind off first 6 (7, 7) sts. Finish row. Turn work.
   - Work across row. Turn work.
   - Bind off 6 (7, 8) sts. Finish row. Turn work.
   - Work across row. Turn work.
   - Bind off last 7 (7, 8) sts.

FRONT

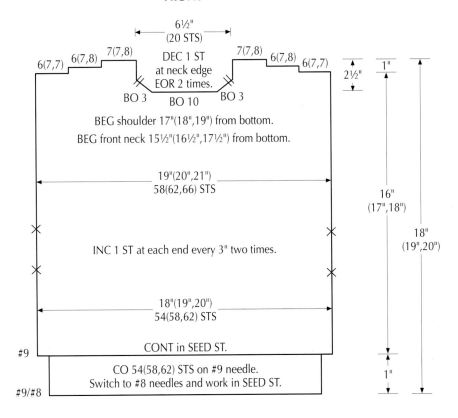

6½"
(20 STS)

6(7,7) 6(7,8) 7(7,8) DEC 1 ST at neck edge EOR 2 times. 7(7,8) 6(7,8) 6(7,7)

2½"   1"

BO 3   BO 10   BO 3

BEG shoulder 17"(18",19") from bottom.
BEG front neck 15½"(16½",17½") from bottom.

19"(20",21")
58(62,66) STS

16"
(17",18")

18"
(19",20")

INC 1 ST at each end every 3" two times.

18"(19",20")
54(58,62) STS

CONT in SEED ST.

#9

CO 54(58,62) STS on #9 needle.
Switch to #8 needles and work in SEED ST.

#9/#8

1"

Sleeves

1. With #9 needles, cast on 28 (30, 32) sts and switch immediately to #8 needles. Work in seed st for 1".
2. Switch to #9 needles and cont in seed st; inc 1 st at each end every 1" 12 times [52 (54, 56) sts; 17" (18", 19") wide].
3. Cont until work measures 16" (17", 18") from bottom.
4. Beg sleeve-cap shaping:
   ◆ Bind off 3 (4, 4) sts at beg of next 2 rows.
   ◆ Bind off 4 (4, 4) sts at beg of next 6 rows.
   ◆ Bind off 4 (4, 5) sts at beg of next 2 rows.
   ◆ Bind off last 14 sts.

Finishing

1. Sew shoulder seams.
2. Neckband: With RS facing and #8 circular needle, pick up a total of 58 sts:
   ◆ 22 sts across back neck from shoulder to shoulder
   ◆ 36 sts across front neck from shoulder to shoulder
   ◆ Work in seed st for 3". Bind off in pattern.
3. Sew in sleeve caps; sew side and sleeve seams.
4. Block assembled sweater to desired measurements.
5. Stabilize back neck and shoulders.

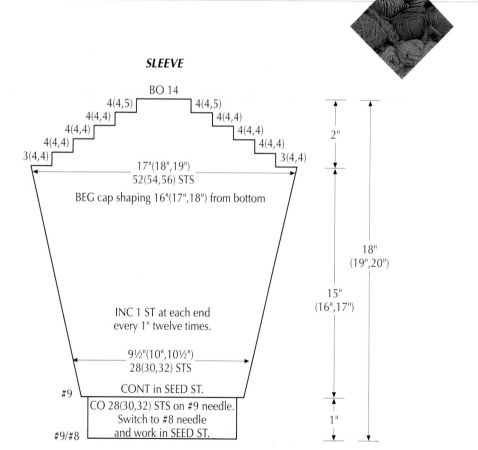

SLEEVE

BO 14

4(4,5)   4(4,5)
4(4,4)   4(4,4)
4(4,4)   4(4,4)
4(4,4)   4(4,4)
3(4,4)   3(4,4)

17"(18",19")
52(54,56) STS

BEG cap shaping 16"(17",18") from bottom

2"

INC 1 ST at each end every 1" twelve times.

18" (19",20")

15" (16",17")

9½"(10",10½")
28(30,32) STS

CONT in SEED ST.

#9

CO 28(30,32) STS on #9 needle. Switch to #8 needle and work in SEED ST.

#9/#8

1"

EASY BASIC PULLOVER

This cropped pullover is even more simple to knit than the previous seed stitch version—the difference is in the stitch. The simple stockinette stitch couldn't be easier and really shows off the beautiful, subtle hand-dyed variation of colors in the yarn. This is a favorite "first sweater" for many beginning knitting students. It knits up quickly, requires very little shaping, and has lots of style!

Size

Small (Medium, Large)
Finished Bust: 38" (40", 42")
Finished Length: 18" (19½", 21")

Materials

Use a yarn that knits at 2.2 sts to 1".
2 (2, 3) skeins of Prism Krinkle, each
  approximately 250 yds. [450 (500,
  550) yds. total]
#10¾ and #11 needles
#10¾ circular needle

Gauge

9 sts and 16 rows = 4" in reverse St st
  using #11 needles
Always check gauge before starting
  sweater. Increase or decrease
  needle size to obtain correct gauge.

Rib Pattern Stitch

Multiple of 4, plus edge stitches:
Row 1 (WS): K1, *K2, P2, rep from
  *, end K1.
On remaining rows, work stitches as
  they face you, remembering to knit
  the edge stitches (page 133).

Back

1. With #10¾ needles, cast on
   38 (42, 42) sts. Work in rib stitch
   for 1".
2. Switch to #11 needles and work in
   St st. On size small and large only:
   Inc 1 st at each end on next row.
   Cont in St st; inc 1 st at each end
   every 3" 2 times [44 (46, 48) sts;
   19" (20", 21") wide].

3. Cont until work measures 16½"
   (18", 19½") from bottom.
4. Beg back neck and shoulder
   shaping:
   ◆ Bind off first 4 (5, 5) sts. Work
     next 10 (10, 11) sts. Keeping 11
     (11, 12) sts on right-hand needle,
     bind off center 14 sts. Finish row.
     Turn work.
   ◆ Bind off first 4 (5, 5) sts. Finish
     row. Turn work.
   ◆ Dec 1 st at neck edge. Finish
     row. Turn work.
   ◆ Bind off 5 (5, 5) sts. Finish row.
     Turn work.

◆ Work across row. Turn work.
◆ Bind off last 5 (5, 6) sts.
5. Complete back neck and shoulder
   shaping:
   ◆ Join yarn at neck edge. Dec 1 st
     and finish row. Turn work.
   ◆ Bind off 5 (5, 5) sts. Finish row.
     Turn work.
   ◆ Work across row. Turn work.
   ◆ Bind off last 5 (5, 6) sts.

BACK

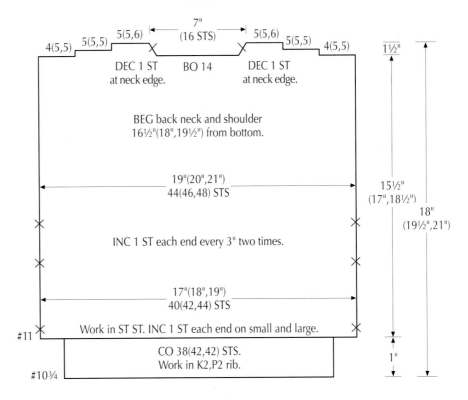

Front

1. Work the front exactly the same as the back until work measures 15" (16½", 18") from bottom.

2. Beg front neck shaping:
   - Work first 17 (18, 19) sts. Bind off center 10 sts. Finish row. Turn work.
   - Work across row. Turn work.
   - Bind off 2 sts at neck edge. Finish row. Turn work.
   - Work across row. Turn work.
   - Dec 1 st at neck edge. Finish row. Turn work.

3. Cont until work measures 16½" (18", 19½") from bottom.

4. Beg shoulder shaping:
   - Beg at outside edge, bind off first 4 (5, 5) sts. Finish row. Turn work.
   - Work across row. Turn work.
   - Bind off 5 (5, 5) sts. Finish row. Turn work.
   - Work back across row. Turn work.
   - Bind off last 5 (5, 6) sts.

5. Complete front neck shaping:
   - Join yarn at neck edge. Bind off first 2 sts. Finish row. Turn work.
   - Work across row. Turn work.
   - Dec 1 st at neck edge. Finish row. Turn work.

6. Cont until work measures 16½" (18", 19½") from bottom.

7. Complete shoulder shaping:
   - Beg at outside edge, bind off first 4 (5, 5) sts. Finish row. Turn work.
   - Work across row. Turn work.
   - Bind off 5 (5, 5) sts. Finish row. Turn work.
   - Work across row. Turn work.
   - Bind off last 5 (5, 6) sts.

FRONT

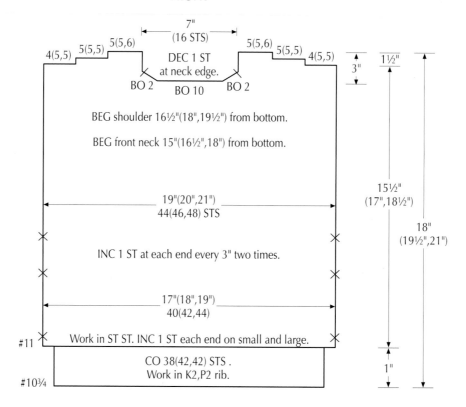

7" (16 STS)

4(5,5) 5(5,5) 5(5,6)   DEC 1 ST at neck edge.   5(5,6) 5(5,5) 4(5,5)

BO 2   BO 10   BO 2

3"   1½"

BEG shoulder 16½"(18",19½") from bottom.

BEG front neck 15"(16½",18") from bottom.

19"(20",21")
44(46,48) STS

15½" (17",18½")

INC 1 ST at each end every 3" two times.

18" (19½",21")

17"(18",19")
40(42,44)

#11   Work in ST ST. INC 1 ST each end on small and large.

CO 38(42,42) STS.
Work in K2,P2 rib.

#10¾

1"

Sleeves

1. With #10³/₄ needles, cast on 18 (22, 22) sts. Work in K2, P2 rib for 1", remembering to knit edge stitches.
2. Switch to #11 needles and work in St st. On size small and large only: Inc 1 st at each end of next row. Cont in St st; inc 1 st at each end every 6 rows 9 times [38 (40, 42) sts; 17" (18", 19") wide].
3. Cont until work measures 16" (17", 18") from bottom.
4. Beg sleeve-cap shaping:

◆ Bind off 3 (3, 3) sts at beg of next 2 rows.
◆ Bind off 3 (4, 4) sts at beg of next 2 rows.
◆ Bind off 4 (4, 5) sts at beg of next 2 rows.
◆ Bind off 5 (5, 5) sts at beg of next 2 rows.
◆ Bind off last 8 sts.

Finishing

1. Sew shoulder seams.
2. Neckband: With RS facing and #10³/₄ circular needle, pick up a total of 52 sts.

◆ 22 sts across back neck
◆ 30 sts across front neck
◆ Work in K2, P2 rib for 2¹/₂", remembering to knit edge stitches.
◆ Work in St st for 1¹/₂". Bind off loosely.
3. Sew in sleeve caps; sew side and sleeve seams.
4. Block assembled sweater to desired measurements.
5. Stabilize back neck and shoulder seams.

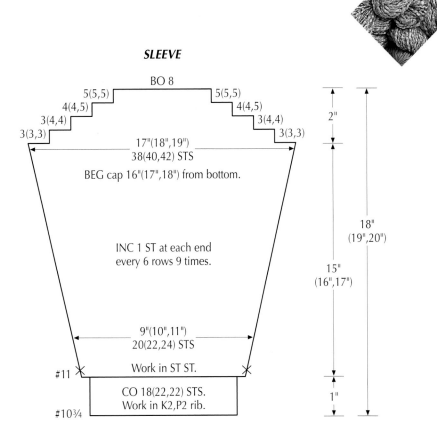

SLEEVE

BO 8

5(5,5)   5(5,5)
4(4,5)   4(4,5)
3(4,4)   3(4,4)
3(3,3)   3(3,3)

17"(18",19")
38(40,42) STS

BEG cap 16"(17",18") from bottom.

2"

INC 1 ST at each end every 6 rows 9 times.

18" (19",20")

15" (16",17")

9"(10",11")
20(22,24) STS

Work in ST ST.

#11

CO 18(22,22) STS.
Work in K2,P2 rib.

#10¾

1"

Ready For Ribbing

RIBBED JACKET

We love the way Stacy Charles develops color "families" that span a broad collection of the Filatura di Crosa yarns each season. They work so beautifully in combination with each other. We designed this sweater to showcase Stacy's beautiful fall collection and developed the black-and-white color work on the collar as a signature detail. The contrast of black and white sets off the rich green palette. Adding an accent of black or navy (depending on which color you wear more often) really "grounds" a sweater and makes it wearable with many pieces already in your closet.

Size

Small (Medium, Large)
Finished Bust: 42" (46", 50")
Finished Length: 19" (21", 23")

Materials

Use the yarns listed in the chart, or a combination of bulky yarns that knit at 3.8 sts to 1". You should have a total of 1825 (1960, 2210) yds.
#5,#6, #7, #8, and #9 needles
5 buttons

Gauge

15 sts and 23 rows = 4" in pattern stitch using #9 needles
Always check gauge before starting sweater. Increase or decrease needle size to obtain correct gauge.

Skeins	Yards	Yarn	Color
1	158	Missoni Rebun	A #456 dk. green
1	158	Missoni Rebun	A #457 dk. green tweed
1 (2, 2)	58 (116, 116)	S. Charles Daniella	B #2 olive/black
2 (2, 3)	186 (186, 279)	Filatura di Crosa Brazza	C #550 olive
1 (1, 2)	66 (66, 132)	Filatura di Crosa Philadelphia	D #459 lime
3 (3, 4)	279 (279, 372)	Filatura di Crosa Brazza	E #532 dk. green
2 (3, 3)	142 (213, 213)	S. Charles Marina	F, J #3 black multi
2	110	Filatura di Corsa Ariete	G #203 dk. green
2	198	Filatura di Crosa Toronto	H #53 lt. green multi
4	176	Filatura di Crosa Sapporo	I #101 lt. green multi
1	66	Filatura di Crosa Philadelphia	K #456 black
1	88	Filatura di Crosa Empire	L #5 black
1	88	Filatura di Crosa Empire	M #1 white

Striping Sequence

No. of Rows	Color	
6	A	#456 dk. green run dbl w/ #457 dk. green tweed
2	B	#2 olive/black
6	C	#550 olive
2	D	#459 lime
8	E	#532 dk. green
3	F	#3 black multi
4	G	#203 dk. green
4	H	#53 lt. green multi
6	I	#101 lt. green multi
2	J	#3 black multi
1	K	#456 black
2-color work	L	#5 black
	M	#1 white

Pattern Stitch

Multiple of 8, plus 2 edge stitches:
Row 1 (WS): K2, *P6, K2, rep from * across row.
Row 2 (RS): K1, P1, *K6, P2, rep from *, end K6, P1, K1.
Repeat rows 1 and 2.

Note: Because ribbing naturally pulls in, you will need to spread your piece a bit; it should "open up" easily and not look distorted to achieve the desired width measurement.

Back

1. With #8 needles, cast on 82 (90, 98) sts. Work in pattern stitch for 2", following striping sequence.

2. Switch to #9 needles and cont in pattern stitch, following striping sequence, until work measures 8$\frac{1}{2}$" (10", 11$\frac{1}{2}$") from bottom [21" (23", 25") wide].

3. Beg armhole shaping:
   ◆ Bind off 6 (7, 8) sts at beg of next 2 rows [70 (76, 82) sts; 18$\frac{1}{2}$" (20", 21$\frac{1}{2}$") wide].

4. Cont until work measures 18" (20", 22") from bottom.

5. Beg back neck and shoulder shaping:
   ◆ Bind off first 5 (6, 7) sts. Knit next 12 (14, 16) sts. Keeping 13 (15, 17) sts on right-hand needle, bind off center 34 sts. Finish row. Turn work.
   ◆ Bind off 5 (6, 7) sts. Finish row. Turn work.
   ◆ Dec 1 st at neck edge. Finish row. Turn work.
   ◆ Bind off 6 (7, 8) sts. Finish row. Turn work.
   ◆ Work across row. Turn work.
   ◆ Bind off last 6 (7, 8) sts.

6. Complete back neck and shoulder shaping:
   ◆ Join yarn at neck edge. Dec 1 st and finish row. Turn work.
   ◆ Bind off 6 (7, 8) sts. Finish row. Turn work.
   ◆ Work across row. Turn work.
   ◆ Bind off last 6 (7, 8) sts.

BACK

9"
(36 STS)

5(6,7)   6(7,8)   6(7,8)   6(7,8)   6(7,8)   5(6,7)

DEC 1 ST   BO 34   DEC 1 ST
at neck edge.   at neck edge.

1"

BEG back neck and shoulder
18"(20",22") from bottom.

9$\frac{1}{2}$"
(10",10$\frac{1}{2}$")

18$\frac{1}{2}$"(20",21$\frac{1}{2}$")
70(76,82) STS

BO 6(7,8)   BO 6(7,8)

BEG armhole 8$\frac{1}{2}$"(10",11$\frac{1}{2}$") from bottom.

19"
(21",23")

6$\frac{1}{2}$"
(8",9$\frac{1}{2}$")

21"(23",25")
82(90,98) STS

CONT in pattern.

#9

CO 82(90,98) STS. See text for setting up pattern.

2"

#8

49

Fronts

1. With #8 needles, cast on 38 (41, 46) sts. Work in pattern stitch for 2", following striping sequence. Work right and left fronts (refers to your right and left sides):
   - ◆ For Small and Large right front:
     Row 1 (WS): K2, *P6, K2, rep from *, end P3, K1.
     Row 2 (RS): K4, *P2, K6, rep from *, end P1, K1.
     Repeat rows 1 and 2.
   - ◆ For Small and Large left front:
     Row 1 (WS): K1, P3, *K2, P6, rep from *, end K2.
     Row 2 (RS): K1, P1, *K6, P2, rep from *, end K4.
     Repeat rows 1 and 2.
   - ◆ For Medium left and right fronts:
     Row 1 (WS):*K2, P6, rep from *, end K1.
     Row 2 (RS): K1, *K6, P2, rep from *, end P1, K1.
     Repeat rows 1 and 2.
2. Switch to #9 needles and cont in pattern stitch until work measures $8\frac{1}{2}$" (10", $11\frac{1}{2}$") from bottom.
3. Beg armhole shaping:
   - ◆ Bind off 6 (7, 8) sts at beg of row [32 (34, 38) sts; 8" (9", 10") wide].
4. Cont until work measures 16" (18", 20") from bottom.
5. Beg front neck shaping:
   - ◆ Beg at neck edge, bind off first 6 sts. Finish row. Turn work.
   - ◆ Work across row. Turn work.
   - ◆ Bind off 3 sts at neck edge. Finish row. Turn work.
   - ◆ Work across row. Turn work.
   - ◆ Dec 1 st at neck edge EOR 3 times.
6. Cont until work measures 18" (20", 22") from bottom.
7. Beg shoulder shaping:
   - ◆ Bind off first 5 (6, 7) sts at outside edge. Finish row. Turn work.
   - ◆ Work across row. Turn work.
   - ◆ Bind off 6 (7, 8) sts. Finish row. Turn work.
   - ◆ Work across row. Turn work.
   - ◆ Bind off last 6 (7, 8) sts.
8. Work second front the same as the right front, but reverse the shaping.

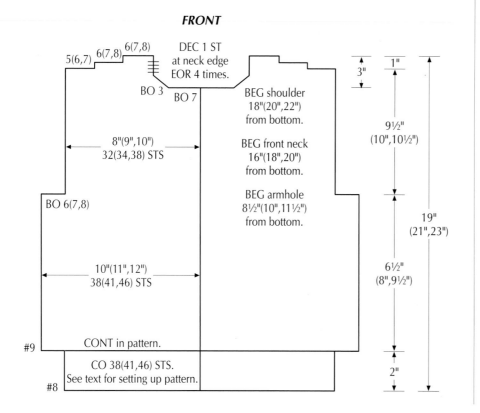

FRONT

5(6,7) 6(7,8) 6(7,8)

DEC 1 ST at neck edge EOR 4 times.

BO 3   BO 7

BEG shoulder 18"(20",22") from bottom.

BEG front neck 16"(18",20") from bottom.

BEG armhole $8\frac{1}{2}$"(10",$11\frac{1}{2}$") from bottom.

8"(9",10") 32(34,38) STS

BO 6(7,8)

10"(11",12") 38(41,46) STS

#9 CONT in pattern.

CO 38(41,46) STS. See text for setting up pattern.

#8

1"

3"

$9\frac{1}{2}$" (10",$10\frac{1}{2}$")

19" (21",23")

$6\frac{1}{2}$" (8",$9\frac{1}{2}$")

2"

Sleeves

1. With #7 needles, cast on 36 (38, 40) sts. Work in pattern stitch for 2", following striping sequence.
   - ◆ For Small:
     Row 1 (WS): K1, P4, *K2, P6, rep from *, end K2, P4, K1.
     Row 2 (RS): K5, *P2, K6, rep from *, end P2, K5.
     Repeat rows 1 and 2.
   - ◆ For Medium:
     Row 1 (WS): K1, P5, *K2, P6, rep from *, end P5, K1.
     Row 2 (RS): K6, *P2, K6, rep from *.
     Repeat rows 1 and 2.
   - ◆ For Large:
     Row 1 (WS): K1, P6, *K2, P6, rep from *, end K1.
     Row 2 (RS): K7, *P2, K6, rep from *, end K1.
     Repeat rows 1 and 2.
2. Switching to #9 needles, work increases into stitch pattern:
   - ◆ Inc 1 st at each end every 4 rows 17 (18, 19) times [70, (74, 78) sts; 18" (19", 20") wide].
3. Cont until work measures 18" (19", 20") from bottom.
4. Beg sleeve-cap shaping:
   - ◆ Bind off 4 (4, 5) sts at beg of next 2 rows.
   - ◆ Bind off 4 (5, 5) sts at beg of next 4 rows.
   - ◆ Bind off 5 (5, 5) sts at beg of next 4 rows.
   - ◆ Bind off 5 (5, 6) sts at beg of next 2 rows.
   - ◆ Bind off last 16 sts.

SLEEVE

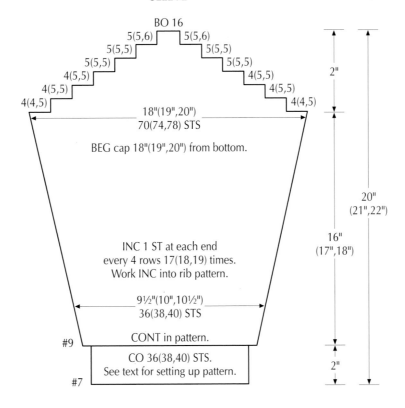

BO 16
5(5,6)   5(5,6)
5(5,5)   5(5,5)
5(5,5)   5(5,5)
4(5,5)   4(5,5)
4(5,5)   4(5,5)
4(4,5)   4(4,5)

18"(19",20")
70(74,78) STS

BEG cap 18"(19",20") from bottom.

2"

20"
(21",22")

16"
(17",18")

INC 1 ST at each end
every 4 rows 17(18,19) times.
Work INC into rib pattern.

9½"(10",10½")
36(38,40) STS

#9   CONT in pattern.

CO 36(38,40) STS.
See text for setting up pattern.

#7

2"

Finishing

1. Because this is a ribbed sweater, steam each piece to size before sewing the garment together. "Opening up" the pieces will help ensure a better fit and make it easier to sew the pieces together.

2. Sew shoulder seams.

3. Front bands: With RS facing and #7 needles, pick up 60 (68, 76) sts. Work in K2, P2 rib for 2", remembering to knit edge stitches.
   - On buttonhole side, work 5 buttonholes in 5th row of rib, spacing them evenly between bottom edge and neck.

4. Collar: With RS facing and #6 needles, pick up a total of 93 sts around neck with color E:
   - 31 sts from center of buttonhole band to shoulder seam
   - 31 sts from shoulder seam to shoulder seam
   - 31 sts from shoulder seam to center of button band

5. Following the color chart above, complete 10 rows of two-color work with colors L and M.

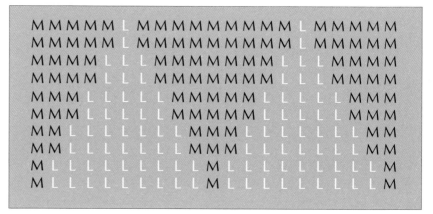

```
M M M M M L M M M M M M M M M L M M M M M
M M M M M L M M M M M M M M M L M M M M M
M M M M L L L M M M M M M M L L L M M M M
M M M M L L L M M M M M M M L L L M M M M
M M M L L L L L M M M M M L L L L L M M M
M M M L L L L L M M M M M L L L L L M M M
M M L L L L L L L M M M L L L L L L L M M
M M L L L L L L L M M M L L L L L L L M M
M L L L L L L L L L M L L L L L L L L L M
M L L L L L L L L L M L L L L L L L L L M
```

6. To finish the collar, work 2 rows in St st with color E.
   - Switch to #5 needles and work 2 more rows in St st with color E.
   - Switch to color L and decrease 9 sts evenly across the next row.
   - Cont in St st on #5 needles in color L for 10 more rows. Bind off.
   - Fold collar to inside and stitch down to create stand-up collar as in photograph.

7. Sew in sleeve caps; sew side and sleeve seams.

8. Sew on buttons to correspond with buttonholes.

9. Block assembled sweater to desired measurements.

10. Stabilize back neck and shoulders.

RIBBED PULLOVER

This is the same basic body shape as the ribbed jacket, but this is the "foolproof" version for those who are a little timid or unsure about pulling together a group of yarns. This version was knit with one beautiful, variegated yarn. All the wonderful color transitions happen as you knit with a single skein! This sweater illustrates perfectly the beauty of variegated fibers. The "split rib" collar adds style and is very easy to execute. If you prefer a longer sweater, simply add the additional length before the armhole shaping begins.

Size

Small (Medium, Large)
Finished Bust: 44" (48", 52")
Finished Length: 19" (21", 23")

Materials

*Use a bulky yarn that knits at 3 sts
to 1".*
6 (7, 8) skeins of Noro Iro, each
approximately 130 yds. [800 (900,
1000) yds. total]
#10$^{1}/_{2}$ and #10$^{3}/_{4}$ needles
#10, #10$^{1}/_{2}$, and #10$^{3}/_{4}$ circular
needles (all 24")
Stitch markers

Gauge

12 sts and 17 rows = 4" in pattern
stitch using #10$^{3}/_{4}$ needles
Always check gauge before starting
sweater. Increase or decrease
needle size to obtain correct gauge.

Front and Back Pattern Stitch

Multiple of 8, plus 8, plus 2 edge
stitches:
Row 1 (WS): K2, *P6, K2, rep from *,
end P6, K2.
Row 2 (RS): K1, P1, *K6, P2, rep from
*, end K6, P1, K1.
Repeat rows 1 and 2.

*Note: Because ribbing naturally pulls in,
you will need to spread your piece a bit;
it should "open up" easily and not look
distorted to achieve the desired width
measurement.*

Back

1. With #10$^{1}/_{2}$ needles, cast on 66 (74,
   82) sts. Work in pattern stitch for 2".

2. Switch to #10$^{3}/_{4}$ needles and cont
   in pattern stitch until work
   measures 8$^{1}/_{2}$" (10", 11$^{1}/_{2}$") from
   bottom [22" (24", 26") wide].
3. Beg armhole shaping:
   ◆ Bind off 7 sts at beg of next 2
   rows [52 (60, 68) sts; 17$^{1}/_{2}$"
   (20", 22$^{1}/_{2}$") wide].
4. Cont until work measures 18"
   (20", 22") from bottom.
5. Beg back neck and shoulder
   shaping:
   ◆ Bind off first 4 (6, 7) sts. Work
   next 10 (12, 15) sts. Keeping 11
   (13, 16) sts on right-hand needle,
   bind off center 22 sts. Finish row.
   Turn work.

◆ Bind off first 4 (6, 7) sts. Finish
row. Turn work.
◆ Dec 1 st at neck edge. Finish
row. Turn work.
◆ Bind off 5 (6, 7) sts. Finish row.
Turn work.
◆ Work across row. Turn work.
◆ Bind off last 5 (6, 8) sts.
6. Complete back neck and shoulder
shaping:
   ◆ Join yarn at neck edge. Dec 1 st
   and finish row. Turn work.
   ◆ Bind off 5 (6, 7) sts. Finish row.
   Turn work.
   ◆ Work across row. Turn work.
   ◆ Bind off last 5 (6, 8) sts.

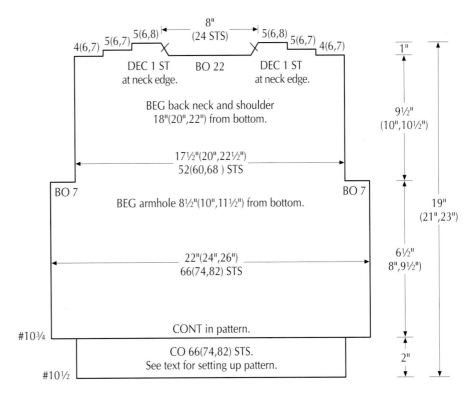

BACK

4(6,7) 5(6,7) 5(6,8) 8" (24 STS) 5(6,8) 5(6,7) 4(6,7)

DEC 1 ST at neck edge.   BO 22   DEC 1 ST at neck edge.

BEG back neck and shoulder
18"(20",22") from bottom.

17$^{1}/_{2}$"(20",22$^{1}/_{2}$")
52(60,68) STS

BO 7   BO 7

BEG armhole 8$^{1}/_{2}$"(10",11$^{1}/_{2}$") from bottom.

22"(24",26")
66(74,82) STS

#10$^{3}/_{4}$ CONT in pattern.

#10$^{1}/_{2}$ CO 66(74,82) STS.
See text for setting up pattern.

1"

9$^{1}/_{2}$"
(10",10$^{1}/_{2}$")

19"
(21",23")

6$^{1}/_{2}$"
8",9$^{1}/_{2}$")

2"

Front

1. Work the front exactly the same as the back until work measures 16" (18", 20") from bottom.
2. Beg front neck shaping:
   - Work first 20 (24, 28) sts. Bind off center 12 sts. Finish row. Turn work.
   - Work across row. Turn work.
   - Bind off first 3 sts at neck edge. Finish row. Turn work.
   - Work across row. Turn work.
   - Dec 1 st at neck edge EOR 3 times.
3. Cont until work measures 18" (20", 22") from bottom.
4. Complete shoulder shaping:
   - Beg at outside edge, bind off first 4 (6, 7) sts. Finish row. Turn work.
   - Work across row. Turn work.
   - Bind off 5 (6, 7) sts. Finish row. Turn work.
   - Work across row. Turn work.
   - Bind off last 5 (6, 8) sts.
5. Complete front neck shaping:
   - Join yarn at neck edge. Bind off first 3 sts. Finish row. Turn work.
   - Work across row. Turn work.
   - Dec 1 st at neck edge EOR 3 times.
6. Cont until work measures 18" (20", 22") from bottom.
7. Complete shoulder shaping:
   - Beg at outside edge, bind off first 4 (6, 7) sts. Finish row. Turn work.
   - Work across row. Turn work.
   - Bind off 5 (6, 7) sts. Finish row. Turn work.
   - Work across row. Turn work.
   - Bind off last 5 (6, 8) sts.

Sleeve Pattern Stitch

Multiple of 8, plus 6, plus 2 edge stitches:
Row 1 (WS): K1, P2, K2, *P6, K2, rep from *, end P2, K1.
Row 2 (RS): K3, *P2, K6, rep from *, end P2, K3.
Repeat rows 1 and 2.

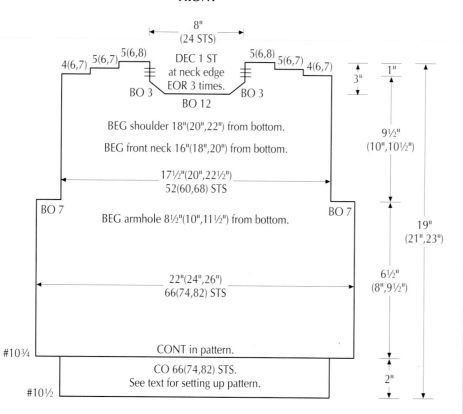

FRONT

Sleeve

1. With #10 1/2 needles, cast on 32 sts. Work in pattern stitch for 2".
2. Switch to #10 3/4 needles and work in pattern stitch; inc 1 st at each end every 4 rows 12 (13, 14) times [56 (58, 60) sts; 18" (19", 20") wide].
3. Cont until work measures 17" (18", 19") from bottom.
4. Beg sleeve-cap shaping:
   - Bind off 6 sts at beg of next 6 rows.
   - Bind off 5 sts at beg of next 2 rows.
   - Bind off last 10 (12, 14) sts.

Finishing

1. Because this is a ribbed sweater, steam each piece to size before sewing the garment together. "Opening up" the pieces will help ensure a better fit and make it easier to sew the pieces together.
2. Sew shoulder seams.
3. Collar: Count halfway across front of sweater and fasten a safety pin. With RS facing and a #10 circular needle, pick up a total of 61 sts:
   - 18 sts from center front to shoulder seam
   - 25 sts from shoulder seam to shoulder seam
   - 18 sts from shoulder seam to center front
   - Work in K1, P1 rib in the round for 1". To set up the split in the front of the collar at this point, place a marker at the center front and work a knit stitch on either side of it.
   - Switch to #10 1/2 circular needle and separate the rib at the front between the two knit sts. To do this, work in pattern around the row to this point, then turn work at the first of the two knit sts and work back in the opposite direction all around the neck to the other front. Continue back and forth in this manner for 1".

(Always knit the first and last stitches in the front. These are now your edge stitches.)
   - At 2" from pick-up row, switch to #10 3/4 circular needle and work in K1, P1 rib for another 1 1/2". Bind off loosely in pattern when collar is 3 1/2" tall.
4. Sew in sleeve caps; sew side and sleeve seams.
5. Block assembled sweater to desired measurements.
6. Stabilize back neck and shoulders.

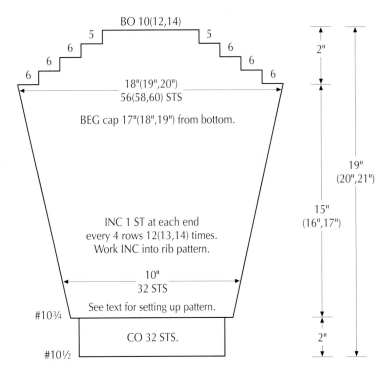

SLEEVE

BO 10(12,14)

5   5
6   6
6   6
6   6

18"(19",20")
56(58,60) STS

BEG cap 17"(18",19") from bottom.

INC 1 ST at each end every 4 rows 12(13,14) times. Work INC into rib pattern.

10"
32 STS

See text for setting up pattern.

#10¾

CO 32 STS.

#10½

2"

19" (20",21")

15" (16",17")

2"

Easy Breezy Tops

CROPPED CARDIGAN

This is an example of a design based on limited materials at hand. Some of our favorite sweaters came about this way. One weekend Lindy flew to California to visit her friend Elisabetta at a remote beach cottage—in other words, no yarn shops! She brought a sweater she wanted to complete for an upcoming trip to the mills in Italy—it was a tricky "brioche" stitch, so she had enough knitting to keep her busy all weekend. But half an hour into her knitting, she tripped over the yarn, pulling out several rows of work. After spending a couple of fruitless hours trying to get the yarn back on the needles, she realized it was hopeless. She needed one of Tricoter's incredible finishers, Ola or Yiming, to sort out the mess. Three days loomed ahead with nothing to knit!

Elisabetta dug around in her closets and drawers, searching for something—anything—to knit. She found a few skeins of a summer cotton, which is usually knit on #5 or #6 needles, but Lindy had only #10 and #10½ needles. After several sketches, swatches, and computations to determine if she had enough yarn, she created this little summer top—knit with the yarn doubled on the needles she'd brought—and wore it home on the plane! Moral of the story: never get caught without a second project because you never know what will happen.

Size

Small (Medium, Large)
Finished Bust: 36" (38", 40")
Finished Length: 15" (16", 17")

Materials

Use two finer yarns that knit together as one, or one bulky yarn that knits at 4.0 sts to 1".

7 (8, 9) skeins of Filatura di Crosa Brilla, each approximately 120 yds. [800 (900, 1000) yds. total if doubled]. If using a single bulky yarn, you will need 450 (550, 650) yds. total.

#10 and #10½ needles
Size I crochet hook
4 buttons

Note: Use unmatched but interesting buttons to add that special finishing touch.

Gauge

16 sts and 18 rows = 4" in pattern stitch using #10½ needles with yarn doubled
Always check gauge before starting sweater. Increase or decrease needle size to obtain correct gauge.

Back Pattern Stitch

Multiple of 4 (including edge stitches):
Row 1 (WS): K3, *P2, K2, rep from *, end P2, K3.
On remaining rows, work stitches as they face you, remembering to always knit the edge stitches (page 133).

Back

1. With #10½ needles, cast on 72 (76, 80) sts using doubled yarn. Work in pattern stitch for 7" (8", 9").
2. Switch to #10 needles. Work in St st and beg armhole shaping:
   - Bind off 3 sts at beg of next 4 rows.
   - Bind off 2 sts at beg of next 6 rows.
   - Dec 1 st at beg of next 8 (12, 16) rows [40 sts; 10" wide].
3. Cont in St st until work measures just short of 15" (16", 17").
4. Beg back neck shaping:
   - Knit first 7 sts. Bind off center 26 sts. Knit last 7 sts. Turn work.
   - Purl across row. Turn work.
   - Dec 1 st at neck edge. Knit across row. Turn work.
   - Bind off last 6 sts.
5. Complete back neck shaping:
   - Join yarn at neck edge. Dec 1 st and finish row. Turn work.
   - Bind off last 6 sts.

BACK

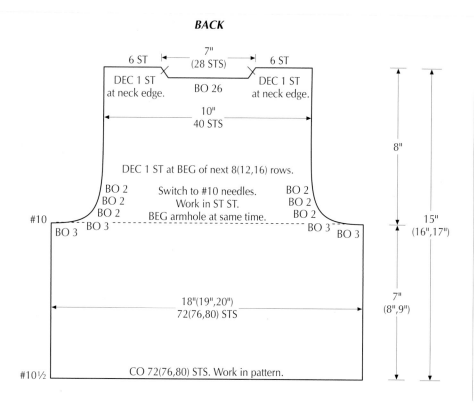

6 ST   7" (28 STS)   6 ST
DEC 1 ST at neck edge.   BO 26   DEC 1 ST at neck edge.
10"
40 STS
DEC 1 ST at BEG of next 8(12,16) rows.
BO 2   Switch to #10 needles.   BO 2
BO 2   Work in ST ST.   BO 2
BO 2   BEG armhole at same time.   BO 2
#10
BO 3   BO 3   BO 3   BO 3
18"(19",20")
72(76,80) STS
#10½   CO 72(76,80) STS. Work in pattern.
8"
15" (16",17")
7" (8",9")

Front Pattern Stitch

Multiple of 4 (including edge stitches):
Row 1 (WS): K1, P2, *K2, P2, rep
   from *, end P2, K1.
On remaining rows, work stitches as
   they face you, remembering to
   always knit the edge stitches.

Fronts

1. With #10½ needles, cast on 36 (40,
   44) sts using doubled yarn. Work
   in pattern stitch for 7", (8", 9").
2. Switch to #10 needles. Work in St
   st and beg armhole shaping:
   • Bind off 3 (5, 5) sts at outside
      edge. Finish row. Turn work.
   • Work across row. Turn work.
   • Bind off 3 (4, 4) sts at outside
      edge. Finish row. Turn work.
   • Work across row. Turn work.
   • Bind off 2 (3, 3) sts at outside
      edge. Finish row. Turn work.
   • Work across row. Turn work.
   • Bind off 2 sts at outside edge
      EOR 2 times.
   • Dec 1 st at outside edge EOR 6
      (6, 10) times.
3. Cont until work measures 11"
   (12", 13").
4. Beg front neck shaping:
   • Bind off 4 sts at neck edge.
      Finish row. Turn work.
   • Work across row. Turn work.
   • Bind off 3 sts at neck edge.
      Finish row. Turn work.
   • Work across row. Turn work.

• Bind off 2 sts at neck edge.
   Finish row. Turn work.
• Work across row. Turn work.
• Dec 1 st at neck edge EOR
   3 times.
5. Cont until work measures 15" (16",
   17") from bottom.
6. Beg at outside edge, bind off last
   6 sts.
7. Work second front the same as first
   front, but reverse the shaping.

Finishing

1. Because this is a ribbed sweater,
   steam each piece to size before
   sewing the garment together.
   "Opening up" the pieces will help
   ensure a better fit and make it
   easier to sew the pieces together.
2. Sew shoulder and side seams.
3. Using doubled yarn, work 1 row
   of single crochet around fronts
   and neck, placing buttonholes as
   desired in this row. Finish with
   1 row of crab stitch (page 140).
4. Complete garment with 1 row of
   single crochet (page 140) and 1
   row of crab stitch around
   armholes.
5. Sew on buttons to correspond with
   buttonholes.
6. Block assembled sweater to
   desired measurements.

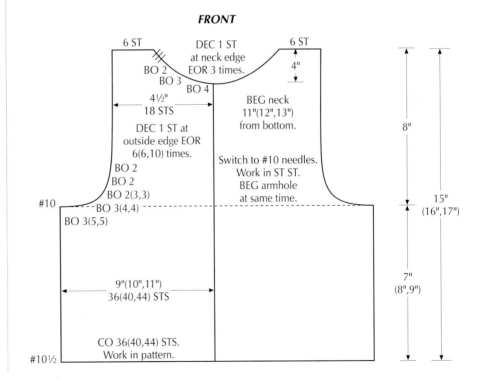

FRONT

6 ST   DEC 1 ST   6 ST
         at neck edge
BO 2   EOR 3 times.   4"
BO 3
         BO 4
4½"   BEG neck
18 STS   11"(12",13")
             from bottom.
DEC 1 ST at
outside edge EOR   Switch to #10 needles.
6(6,10) times.   Work in ST ST.
                     BEG armhole
BO 2   at same time.
BO 2
BO 2(3,3)   8"
#10 --- BO 3(4,4) ------------
BO 3(5,5)   15"
                                             (16",17")
9"(10",11")   7"
36(40,44) STS   (8",9")

CO 36(40,44) STS.
Work in pattern.
#10½

Easy Breezy Tops

STRIPED PULLOVER

The little cardigan became such a favorite at Tricoter that we developed this striped pullover version several seasons later. Both sweaters continue to be popular patterns among our customers, who make them in lots of different summer fibers. You might consider knitting this in metallic yarns for a great little evening sweater to wear for your next black-tie event! Or, what about soft chenille stripes to wear with jeans?

Size

Small (Medium, Large)

Finished Bust: 36" (38", 40")

Finished Length: 15" (16", 17")

Materials

Use two finer yarns that knit together as one, or one bulky yarn that knits at 4.0 sts to 1".

3 (3, 3) skeins each of 3 colors of Filatura de Crosa Brilla, each approximately 120 yds. [800 (900, 1000) yds. total if doubled]. If using a single bulky yarn, you will need 450 (550, 650) yds. total of each color.

#10 and #10½ needles

Size I crochet hook

Gauge

16 sts and 18 rows = 4" in pattern stitch using #10½ needles with yarn doubled

Always check gauge before starting sweater. Increase or decrease needle size to obtain correct gauge.

Striping Sequence

From bottom to armholes, work 4 rows in each of the 3 colors.

From armholes to shoulder, work 2 rows in each of the 3 colors using the same color sequence.

A Red

B Yellow

C Fuchsia

Pattern Stitch

Multiple of 4, plus 2 edge stitches:

Row 1 (WS): K1, *K2, P2, rep from *, end K1.

On remaining rows, work stitches as they face you, remembering to always knit the edge stitches (page 133).

Back

1. With #10½ needles, cast on 74 (78, 82) sts in color A, using doubled yarn. Work in pattern stitch for 7" (8", 9"), following striping sequence.

2. Switch to #10 needles. Work in St st and beg armhole shaping, following striping sequence:
   - Bind off 3 sts at beg of next 4 rows.
   - Bind off 2 sts at beg of next 6 rows.
   - Dec 1 st at beg of next 8 (12, 16) rows (42 sts; 10" wide).

3. Cont until work measures just short of 15" (16", 17").

4. Beg back neck shaping: Turn work
   - Knit first 7 sts. Bind off center 28 sts. Knit last 7 sts. Turn work.
   - Purl across row. Turn work.

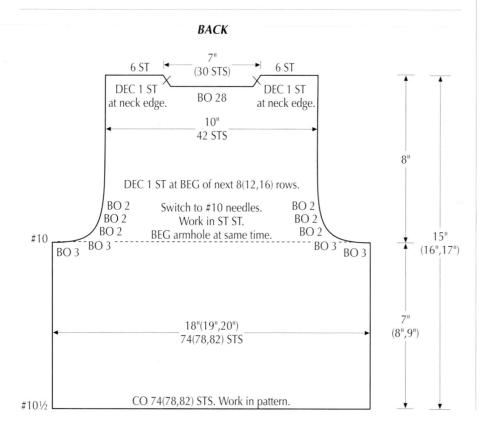

BACK

6 ST | 7" (30 STS) | 6 ST

DEC 1 ST at neck edge. | BO 28 | DEC 1 ST at neck edge.

10" 42 STS

DEC 1 ST at BEG of next 8(12,16) rows.

BO 2 BO 2 BO 2 | Switch to #10 needles. Work in ST ST. BEG armhole at same time. | BO 2 BO 2 BO 2

#10

BO 3 BO 3 | BO 3 BO 3

18"(19",20") 74(78,82) STS

CO 74(78,82) STS. Work in pattern.

#10½

8"

15" (16",17")

7" (8",9")

- ◆ Dec 1 st at neck edge. Knit across row. Turn work.
- ◆ Bind off last 6 sts.
5. Complete back neck shaping:
   - ◆ Join yarn at neck edge. Dec 1 st and finish row. Turn work.
   - ◆ Bind off last 6 sts.

Front

1. Work the front exactly the same as the back until work measures 11" (12", 13") from bottom.
2. Beg front neck shaping:
   - ◆ Knit first 12 sts. Bind off center 18 sts. Knit last 12 sts. Turn work.
   - ◆ Purl across row. Turn work.
   - ◆ Bind off 3 sts at neck edge. Knit across row. Turn work.
   - ◆ Purl across row. Turn work.
   - ◆ Bind off 2 sts at neck edge. Knit across row. Turn work.
   - ◆ Purl across row. Turn work.
   - ◆ Dec 1 st at neck edge. Knit across row. Turn work.
3. Cont until work measures 15" (16", 17") from bottom.

4. Beg at outside edge, bind off last 6 sts.
5. Complete front neck shaping:
   - ◆ Join yarn at neck edge and bind off first 3 sts. Purl across row. Turn work.
   - ◆ Knit across row. Turn work.
   - ◆ Bind off 2 sts at neck edge. Purl across row. Turn work.
   - ◆ Knit across row. Turn work.
   - ◆ Dec 1 st at neck edge. Purl across row. Turn work.
6. Cont until work measures 15" (16", 17") from bottom.
7. Beg at outside edge, bind off last 6 sts.

Finishing

1. Because this is a ribbed sweater, steam each piece to size before sewing the garment together. "Opening up" the pieces will help ensure a better fit and make it easier to sew the pieces together.
2. Sew shoulder and side seams.
3. Using doubled yarn, work 1 row of single crochet and 1 row of crab stitch around the neck and armholes (page 140).
4. Block assembled sweater to desired measurements.

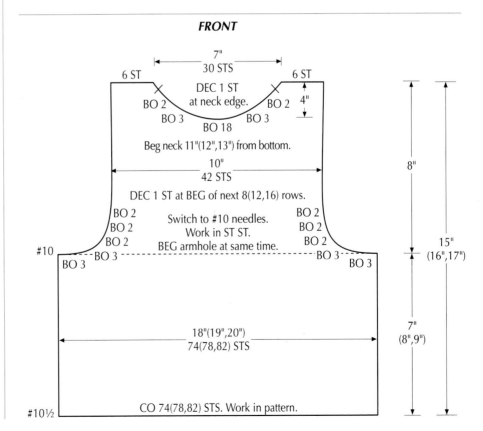

FRONT

7"
30 STS
6 ST   6 ST
BO 2   DEC 1 ST   BO 2   4"
at neck edge.
BO 3   BO 3
BO 18
Beg neck 11"(12",13") from bottom.
10"
42 STS
DEC 1 ST at BEG of next 8(12,16) rows.
BO 2   BO 2   8"
Switch to #10 needles.
BO 2   BO 2
Work in ST ST.
BO 2   BO 2
BEG armhole at same time.
#10   BO 3   BO 3   15"
BO 3   BO 3   (16",17")
18"(19",20")
74(78,82) STS
7"
(8",9")
#10½   CO 74(78,82) STS. Work in pattern.

Simple Summer Shapes
SLEEVELESS CARDIGAN

We scan every new knitting magazine and publication that comes out. We purchase knitting books from many vendors whose yarn we may not carry, just to stay abreast of new sweater shapes. We have a fairly extensive library of publications, dating back several years, and we have even been known to scour thrift shops for really old, out-of-print copies of knitting magazines—often, the silhouettes are as great today as they were when they were first published!

The sweater you see here was inspired by a children's book of summer dresses! We loved the shape of the little bodice and the pattern stitch. We made only a few changes: ribbing at the bottom in place of a skirt and more-adult dimensions. This has become one of our summer favorites, worn either buttoned as a top or left open over a bodysuit as a vest.

Size

Small (Medium, Large)
Finished Bust: 34" (38", 42")
Finished Length: 16" (17", 18")

Materials

*Use a summer yarn that knits at
   5.0 sts to 1".*
6 (7, 8) skeins of Missoni Camogli,
   each approximately 98 yds.
   [625 (725, 825) yds. total]
#3, #4, and #6 needles
5 (6, 7) buttons

Gauge

20 sts and 26 rows = 4" in pattern
   stitch using #6 needles
Always check gauge before starting
   sweater. Increase or decrease
   needle size to obtain correct gauge.

Rib Pattern Stitch for Back

Multiple of 5, plus 2 edge stitches:
Row 1 (WS): K1, *P3, K2, rep from *,
   end K1.
On remaining rows, work stitches as
   they face you, remembering to
always knit the edge stitches
(page 133).

Front and Back Pattern Stitch

Multiple of 5, plus 1 (including edge
   stitches):
Row 1: K1, *K4, SL 1, rep from *,
   end K5.
Row 2: Purl.
Row 3 (and all odd number rows):
   Repeat row 1.
Row 4: Purl.
Row 5: Repeat row 1.
Row 6: K1, *K4, P1, rep from *,
   end K5.
Repeat rows 1–6.

Back

1. With #4 needles, cast on 86 (96,
   106) sts and work in rib pattern
   stitch for 1".
2. Switch to #6 needles and work in
   pattern stitch until work measures
   7½" (8½", 9½") from bottom
   [17" (19", 21") wide].
3. Beg armhole shaping:
   ◆ Bind off 6 sts at beg of next
      2 rows.
   ◆ Bind off 4 sts at beg of next
      2 rows.
   ◆ Bind off 3 sts at beg of next
      2 rows.
   ◆ Bind off 2 sts at beg of next
      2 rows.
   ◆ Dec 1 st at beg of next 10 rows
      [46 (56, 66) sts; 9" (11", 13") wide].

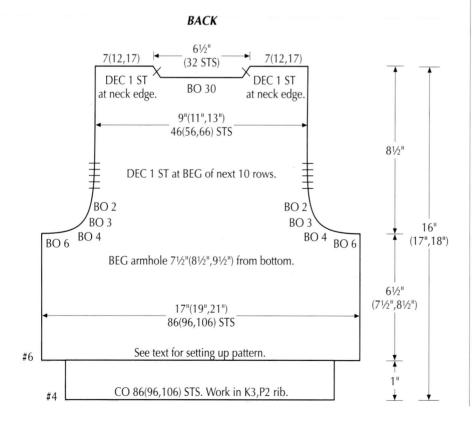

BACK

6½"
(32 STS)

7(12,17)   7(12,17)

DEC 1 ST   BO 30   DEC 1 ST
at neck edge.   at neck edge.

9"(11",13")
46(56,66) STS

DEC 1 ST at BEG of next 10 rows.

BO 2   BO 2
BO 3   BO 3
BO 6 BO 4   BO 4 BO 6

BEG armhole 7½"(8½",9½") from bottom.

17"(19",21")
86(96,106) STS

See text for setting up pattern.

#6

#4   CO 86(96,106) STS. Work in K3,P2 rib.

8½"

16"
(17",18")

6½"
(7½",8½")

1"

4. Cont until work measures just short of 16" (17", 18").

5. Beg back neck shaping:
   ◆ Knit first 8 (13, 18) sts in pattern. Bind off center 30 sts. Finish row. Turn work.
   ◆ Work across row. Turn work.
   ◆ Dec 1 st at neck edge. Finish row. Turn work.
   ◆ Bind off last 7 (12, 17) sts.

6. Complete back neck shaping:
   ◆ Join yarn at neck edge. Dec 1 st and finish row. Turn work.
   ◆ Bind off last 7 (12, 17) sts in pattern.

Rib Pattern Stitch for Front

Multiple of 5, plus 2 edge stitches:
Row 1 (WS): K1, *P2, K3, rep from *, end K1.

On remaining rows, work stitches as they face you, remembering to knit the edge stitches (page 133).

Fronts

1. With #4 needles, cast on 42 (47, 52) sts. Work in rib pattern stitch for 1".
   ◆ Dec 1 st in last row of ribbing.

2. Switch to #6 needles and work in pattern stitch (page 68) until work measures 7½" (8½", 9½") from bottom [41 (46, 51) sts; 8½" (9½", 10½") wide].

3. Beg armhole shaping:
   ◆ Bind off 6 sts at outside edge. Finish row. Turn work.

   ◆ Work across row. Turn work.
   ◆ Bind off 4 sts at outside edge. Finish row. Turn work.
   ◆ Work across row. Turn work.
   ◆ Bind off 3 sts at outside edge. Finish row. Turn work.
   ◆ Work across row. Turn work.
   ◆ Bind off 2 sts at outside edge. Finish row. Turn work.
   ◆ Work across row. Turn work.
   ◆ Dec 1 st at outside edge EOR 3 times.

4. Cont until work measures 10" (11", 12") from bottom [23 (28, 33) sts; 4½" (5½", 6½") wide].

5. Beg front neck shaping:

   ◆ Bind off 3 sts at neck edge. Finish row. Turn work.
   ◆ Work across row. Turn work.
   ◆ Bind off 2 sts at neck edge. Finish row. Turn work.
   ◆ Work across row. Turn work.
   ◆ Dec 1 st at neck edge EOR 11 times.

6. Cont until work measures 16" (17", 18") from bottom.

7. Beg at outside edge, bind off last 7 (12, 17) sts in pattern.

8. Work the second front the same as the first front, but reverse the shaping.

FRONT

7(12,17)   DEC 1 ST at neck edge EOR 11 times.   7(12,17)

6"

BO2   BO3

4½"(5½",6½")
23(28,33) STS

BEG neck 10"(11",12") from bottom.

DEC 1 ST at outside edge EOR 3 times.

BEG armhole 7½"(8½",9½") from bottom.

BO 2
BO 3
BO 4
BO 6

8½"(9½",10½")
41(46,51) STS

8½"

16" (17",18")

6½" (7½",8½")

#6   See text for setting up pattern.

CO 42(47,52) STS.
Work in K3,P2 rib.
DEC 1 ST in last row rib.

#4

1"

Finishing

1. Sew shoulder seams.
2. Front bands: With RS facing and #3 needles, pick up 58 (63, 68) sts for each band.
   - Row 1 (WS): Work in P3, K2 rib for 1". Bind off in pattern. On buttonhole side, work 5 (6, 7) buttonholes in 4th row of ribbing, spacing them evenly between bottom edge and first neck decrease.
3. Collar: With #4 needles, pick up a total of 94 sts:

- 31 sts from lower right front to shoulder seam
- 32 sts across back neck from shoulder to shoulder
- 31 sts from second shoulder seam to lower left front
- Work in rib pattern for 2 1/2". Row 1: K3, *P3, K2, rep from *, end K3. On remaining rows, work stitches as they face you, remembering to knit the edge stitches. Bind off in pattern.

Note: Row 1 is the RS of collar when folded back.

4. Armhole bands: With RS facing and #3 needles, pick up 110 sts for each band.
   - Work in P3, K2 rib for 3/4". Bind off in pattern.
5. Sew side seams.
6. Sew on buttons to correspond with buttonholes.
7. Block assembled sweater to desired measurements.

BACK BUTTON TOP

We loved the small, cropped shape of our sleeveless summer cardigan top, but thought it would be fun to give it a different twist by making it into a little shell that buttons up the back. We created this version without a collar and dropped the shaping on the front and back to the same depth so it could be worn with either the front or the back buttoned. Because this is another one of those quick, easy summer knits, we chose to double the yarn to get it on a bigger needle and used a very easy allover pattern stitch for interest.

Size

Small (Medium, Large)
Finished Bust: 32" (34", 38")
Finished Length: 16" (17", 18")

Materials

*Use two finer yarns that knit together
as one, or one bulky yarn that knits
at 3.5 sts to 1".*
8 (8, 10) skeins of Lang San Remo,
each approximately 115 yds.
[720 (840, 960) yds. total if doubled]
If using a single bulky yarn, you
will need 400 (450, 500) yds. total.
#8 and #10 needles
#8 circular needle (24")
3 stitch holders
6 (6, 7) buttons

Gauge

14 sts and 20 rows = 4" in pattern
stitch using #10 needles with
doubled yarn
Always check gauge before starting
sweater. Increase or decrease
needle size to obtain correct gauge.

Pattern Stitch

Multiple of 4, plus 1, plus 2 edge
stitches:
Row 1 (RS): K1, *P1, K3, rep from *
across row, end P1, K1.
Row 2: Purl.
Row 3: *K3, P1, rep from * across
row, end K3.
Row 4: Purl.
Repeat rows 1–4.

Front

1. With #8 needles, cast on 59
(63, 67) sts using doubled yarn.
Work in K1, P1 rib for 1".
2. Switch to #10 needles and work in
pattern stitch until work measures
7½" (8½", 9½") from bottom
[16" (17", 18") wide].
3. Beg armhole shaping:
   ◆ Bind off 4 sts at beg of next
   2 rows.
   ◆ Bind off 2 sts at beg of next 4
   rows.
   ◆ Dec 1 st at beg of next 8 rows
   [35 (39, 43) sts; 10" (11", 12")
   wide].

4. Cont in pattern stitch until work
measures 12" (13", 14") from
bottom.
5. Beg front neck shaping:
   ◆ Work first 12 (14, 16) sts. Place
   center 11 sts on a holder. Finish
   row. Turn work.
   ◆ Work across row. Turn work.
   ◆ Bind off 2 sts at neck edge.
   Finish row. Turn work.
   ◆ Work across row. Turn work.
   ◆ Bind off 2 sts at neck edge.
   Finish row. Turn work.
   ◆ Work across row. Turn work.
   ◆ Dec 1 st at neck edge EOR 2
   times.

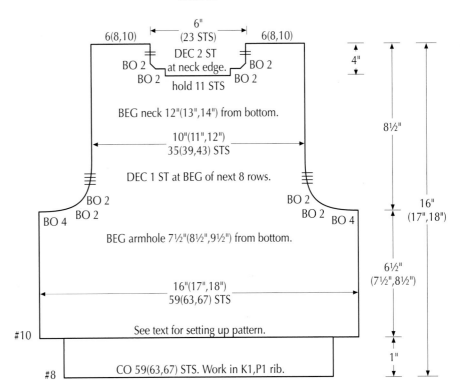

FRONT

6" (23 STS)
6(8,10)   6(8,10)
DEC 2 ST at neck edge.
BO 2   BO 2
BO 2   BO 2
hold 11 STS

BEG neck 12"(13",14") from bottom.

10"(11",12")
35(39,43) STS

4"

8½"

DEC 1 ST at BEG of next 8 rows.

BO 2   BO 2
BO 4 BO 2   BO 2 BO 4

BEG armhole 7½"(8½",9½") from bottom.

16"(17",18")
59(63,67) STS

16" (17",18")

6½" (7½",8½")

See text for setting up pattern.

#10

CO 59(63,67) STS. Work in K1,P1 rib.

#8

1"

6. Cont until work measures 16" (17", 18") from bottom.

7. Beg at outside edge, bind off last 6 (8, 10) sts.

8. Complete front neck shaping:
   - Join yarn at neck edge and bind off first 2 sts. Finish row. Turn work.
   - Work across row. Turn work.
   - Bind off 2 sts at neck edge. Finish row. Turn work.
   - Work across row. Turn work.
   - Dec 1 st at neck edge EOR 2 times.

9. Cont until work measures 16" (17", 18") from bottom.

10. Beg at outside edge, bind off last 6 (8, 10) sts.

Backs

1. With #8 needles, cast on 27 (31, 35) sts using doubled yarn. Work in K1, P1 rib for 1".

2. Switch to #10 needles and work in pattern stitch until work measures 7½" (8½", 9½") from bottom [7" (8", 9") wide].

3. Beg armhole shaping:
   - Bind off 4 sts at outside edge. Finish row. Turn work.
   - Work across row. Turn work.
   - Bind off 2 sts at outside edge. Finish row. Turn work.
   - Work across row. Turn work.
   - Bind off 2 sts at outside edge. Finish row. Turn work.
   - Work across row. Turn work.
   - Dec 1 st at outside edge EOR 4 times [15 (19, 23) sts; 4½" (5½", 6½") wide].

4. Cont until work measures 12" (13", 14") from bottom.

5. Beg back neck shaping:
   - Place first 4 (6, 8) sts on a holder. Finish row. Turn work.
   - Work across row. Turn work.
   - Bind off 2 sts at neck edge. Finish row. Turn work.
   - Work across row. Turn work.
   - Bind off 2 sts at neck edge. Finish row. Turn work.
   - Work across row. Turn work.
   - Dec 1 st at neck edge. Finish row. Turn work.
   - Work across row. Turn work.

6. Cont until work measures 16" (17", 18") from bottom.

7. Beg at outside edge, bind off last 6 (8, 10) sts.

8. Work second back the same as first, but reverse the shaping.

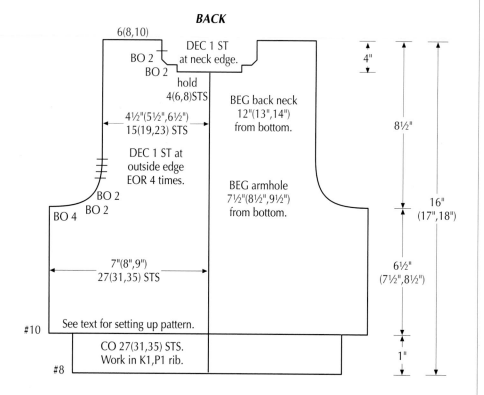

BACK

6(8,10)

BO 2

BO 2

DEC 1 ST at neck edge.

hold 4(6,8)STS

4½"(5½",6½") 15(19,23) STS

DEC 1 ST at outside edge EOR 4 times.

BO 2

BO 4 BO 2

7"(8",9") 27(31,35) STS

#10 See text for setting up pattern.

#8 CO 27(31,35) STS. Work in K1,P1 rib.

BEG back neck 12"(13",14") from bottom

BEG armhole 7½"(8½",9½") from bottom.

4"

8½"

16" (17",18")

6½" (7½",8½")

1"

Finishing

1. Sew shoulder seams.
2. Neckband: With RS facing and #8 circular needle, pick up a total of 79 sts (including the ones on the stitch holders as you come to them) using doubled yarn.
   - 18 sts from left front to shoulder seam
   - 44 sts from shoulder seam to shoulder seam across front neck
   - 18 sts from shoulder seam to right front
   - Work 3 rows in K1, P1 rib and bind off in pattern.
3. Back button bands: With RS facing and #8 needles, pick up 45 (49, 53) sts using doubled yarn.
   - Work 3 rows in K1, P1 rib. On buttonhole side, work 6 (6, 7) buttonholes in second row of ribbing.
   - Work 2 more rows in K1, P1 rib. Bind off in pattern.
4. Armhole bands: With RS facing and #8 needles, pick up 68 sts for each band using doubled yarn.
   - Work 3 rows in K1, P1 rib. Bind off in pattern.
5. Sew side seams.
6. Sew on buttons to correspond with buttonholes.
7. Block assembled sweater to desired measurements.

Terrific Tees

STRIPED TEE-SHIRT

We have found that some of the most spectacular sweaters are the simplest to make, and this is a good example. The particular fiber we chose is called Cool Stuff—and it certainly is! It was created by our good friend Laura Bryant, the owner of a company called Prism and one of the creative geniuses of the yarn industry. Laura develops color families of yarns in a variety of textures and then combines them by hand tying every five yards or so to create some of the most incredible skeins of yarn imaginable. This particular sweater used a color called Cantina and spans the entire color spectrum once in each 30-yard skein!

There are many great alternatives. You could select your own group of yarns and change fibers every few rows randomly to create a similar effect.

Size

Small (Medium, Large)
Finished Bust: 40" (44", 48")
Finished Length: 19½" (21", 23")

Materials

Use a yarn that knits at 4.0 sts to 1".
2 (3, 3) skeins of Prism Cool Stuff,
  each approximately 300 yds. [600
  (800, 900) yds. total]
50 yds. of a complementary yarn or
  ribbon for crochet edging
#8 needles
Size H crochet hook

Gauge

16 sts and 22 rows = 4" in St st using
  #8 needles
Always check gauge before starting
  sweater. Increase or decrease
  needle size to obtain correct gauge.

Cable Cast-on

The cable cast-on is wonderful for its
reversibility. It produces a smooth,
twisted-cable effect on the lower
edge, viewed from either side.
Because it is not very elastic, this cast-
on method is best suited for pieces
that do not require an elastic edge.

1. Insert the right needle between
   the 1st and 2nd sts; wrap it as if
   to knit.

2. Pull the loop forward.

3. Place the loop on the left-hand
   needle. Cont in this fashion,
   working between the last 2 stitches
   on the needle, until you have the
   desired number of stitches.

If you insert the right-hand needle
between the two stitches before you
pull the working yarn for tension, you
will have no trouble inserting the
needle, and your tension will be more
uniform.

Back and Front

Both back and front pieces are
worked the same.

1. With #8 needles, cast on 74
   (82, 90) sts. Work in St st for 2".

2. Cont in St st; inc 1 st at each end
   every 2" 3 times [80 (88, 96) sts;
   (20" (22", 24") wide].

3. Cont until work measures 8½"
   (10", 11½") from bottom.

4. Beg sleeve shaping:
   ◆ Inc 1 st at beg of next 8 rows.
   ◆ Cast on 8 sts at beg of next
     2 rows (see cable cast-on
     directions).
   ◆ Cast on 10 sts at beg of next
     2 rows [124 (132, 140) sts;
     31" (33", 35") wide].

5. Cont until work measures 17½"
   (19", 21") from bottom.

6. Work neck and shoulder shaping
   at the same time:
   ◆ Bind off 8 (9, 10) sts. Knit 45
     (48, 51) sts. Keeping 46 (49, 52)
     sts on right-hand needle, bind off
     center 16 sts. Finish row.
     Turn work.
   ◆ Bind off 8 (9, 10) sts. Work across
     row. Turn work.
   ◆ Bind off 4 sts at neck edge.
     Finish row. Turn work.
   ◆ Bind off 9 (9, 10) sts. Work across
     row. Turn work.
   ◆ Bind off 2 sts at neck edge.
     Finish row. Turn work.
   ◆ Bind off 9 (10, 10) sts. Work
     across row. Turn work.
   ◆ Bind off 2 sts at neck edge.
     Finish row. Turn work.

- Bind off 9 (10, 11) sts. Work across row. Turn work.
- Bind off 2 sts at neck edge. Finish row. Turn work.
- Bind off last 9 (10, 11) sts.
7. Complete the other side of your piece:
  - Join yarn at neck edge (on the purl side) and bind off 4 sts. Purl across row. Turn work.
  - Bind off 9 (9, 10) sts. Work across row. Turn work.
  - Bind off 2 sts at neck edge. Finish row. Turn work.

- Bind off 9 (10, 10) sts. Work across row. Turn work.
- Bind off 2 sts at neck edge. Finish row. Turn work.
- Bind off 9 (10, 11) sts. Work across row. Turn work.
- Bind off 2 sts at neck edge. Finish row. Turn work.
- Bind off last 9 (10, 11) sts.
8. Work second piece the same as first.

Finishing

1. Sew shoulder and side seams.

2. To finish the neck and armholes, work 1 row of single crochet and 1 row of crab stitch (page 140). You can use the same yarn as the body of the sweater or select a complementary yarn or ribbon for the crochet.

3. To finish the bottom of the sweater, work 1 row of single crochet.

4. Block assembled sweater to desired measurements.

5. Stabilize shoulders.

BACK / FRONT

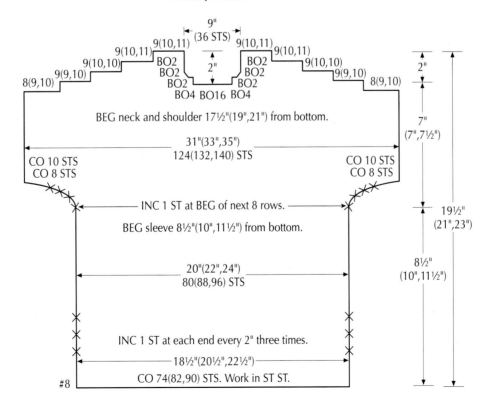

RIBBON TEE-SHIRT

This tee-shirt came about because we just loved the shape and the fit—not to mention the ease of knitting—of our Cool Stuff Tee-shirt. We wanted just such a simple shape to show off the beauty of the hand-dyed rayon ribbon. This has been the beginning knitting project for countless new knitters who loved the simple pattern, which they could complete in a reasonable amount of time, but who still wanted a sweater that had style. (Particularly for new knitters, success in a first garment is the greatest incentive to continue.) It is literally a weekend project for many people!

When using hand-dyed, variegated yarns, use two skeins, changing skeins every two rows to avoid slight variances in color from one skein to the next.

TRICOTER
Knitting specialists

Size

Small (Medium, Large)
Finished Bust: 38" (42", 46")
Finished Length: 19½" (21", 23")

Materials

Use a yarn that knits at 3.25 sts to 1".
5 (6, 7) skeins of Alfie's Rayon Ribbon, each approximately 100 yds. [450 (550, 650) yds. total]
#11 needles
Size J crochet hook

Gauge

13 sts and 14 rows = 4" in St st using #11 needles
Always check gauge before starting sweater. Increase or decrease needle size to obtain correct gauge.

Back and Front

Both back and front pieces are worked the same.
1. With #11 needles, cast on 56 (62, 68) sts. Work in St st for 2".

BACK / FRONT

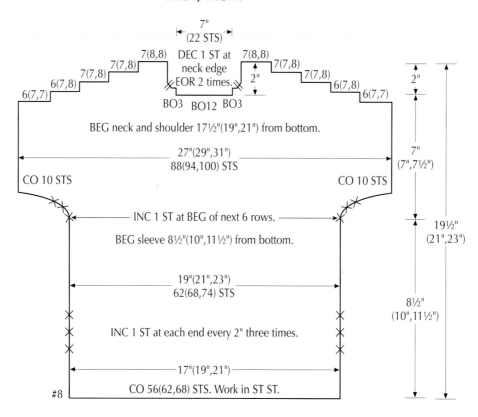

7"
(22 STS)
7(8,8) DEC 1 ST at neck edge EOR 2 times. 7(8,8)
7(7,8) 7(7,8) 7(7,8) 7(7,8)
6(7,8) 6(7,8)
6(7,7) 6(7,7)
2"
BO3 BO12 BO3
BEG neck and shoulder 17½"(19",21") from bottom.
27"(29",31")
88(94,100) STS
CO 10 STS   CO 10 STS
2"
7"
(7",7½")
INC 1 ST at BEG of next 6 rows.
BEG sleeve 8½"(10",11½") from bottom.
19"(21",23")
62(68,74) STS
19½"
(21",23")
INC 1 ST at each end every 2" three times.
8½"
(10",11½")
17"(19",21")
CO 56(62,68) STS. Work in ST ST.
#8

2. Cont in St st, inc 1 st at each end every 2" 3 times [62 (68, 74) sts; 19" (21", 23") wide].

3. Cont until work measures 8¹/₂" (10", 11¹/₂") from bottom.

4. Beg sleeve shaping:
   ◆ Inc 1 st at beg of next 6 rows.
   ◆ Cast on 10 sts at beginning of next 2 rows [88 (94, 100) sts; 28" (31", 33") wide]. (See cable cast-on directions, page 78.)

5. Cont until work measures 17¹/₂" (19", 21") from bottom.

6. Work neck and shoulder shaping at the same time:
   ◆ Bind off 6 (7, 7) sts. Knit 31 (33, 36) sts. Keeping 32 (34, 37) sts on right-hand needle, bind off center 12 sts. Finish row. Turn work.
   ◆ Bind off 6 (7, 7) sts. Work across row. Turn work.
   ◆ Bind off 3 sts at neck edge. Finish row. Turn work.
   ◆ Bind off 6 (7, 8) sts. Work across row. Turn work.
   ◆ Dec 1 st at neck edge. Finish row. Turn work.
   ◆ Bind off 7 (7, 8) sts. Work across row. Turn work.
   ◆ Dec 1 st at neck edge. Finish row. Turn work.
   ◆ Bind off 7 (7, 8) sts. Work across row. Turn work.
   ◆ Work across row. Turn work.
   ◆ Bind off last 7 (8, 8) sts.

7. Complete the other half of neck and shoulder shaping:
   ◆ Join yarn at neck edge (on the purl side). Bind off 3 sts. Work across row. Turn work.
   ◆ Bind off 6 (7, 8) sts. Work across row. Turn work.
   ◆ Dec 1 st at neck edge. Finish row. Turn work.
   ◆ Bind off 7 (7, 8) sts. Work across row. Turn work.
   ◆ Dec 1 st at neck edge. Finish row. Turn work.
   ◆ Bind off 7 (7, 8) sts. Work across row. Turn work.
   ◆ Work across row. Turn work.
   ◆ Bind off last 7 (8, 8) sts.

8. Work second piece the same as first.

Finishing

1. Sew shoulder and side seams.

2. To finish the neck, armholes, and bottom, work 1 row of single crochet and 1 row of crab stitch (page 140). You can use the same yarn as the body of the sweater or select a complementary yarn or ribbon for the crochet.

3. Block assembled sweater to desired measurements.

4. Stabilize shoulders.

Super Summer Cardigans

RIBBED FITTED CARDIGAN

This sweater was inspired by the beautiful hand-dyed yarns from Laura Bryant at Prism. Laura adds several colors to her repertoire each season. The one we used for this sweater is called Nevada. We loved the navy/olive/sienna mix and the wonderful combination of textures that all knit at similar gauges but have completely different looks. We added a couple of complementary solid-color yarns to highlight the hand-dyed fibers. We chose a knit 2, purl 2 ribbing because it added interest without diminishing the beauty of the fibers themselves.

Sleeve Pattern Stitch

Multiple of 4, plus 2, plus 2 edge
stitches:

Row 1 (WS): K1, *K2, P2, rep from *,
end K2, K1.

On remaining rows, work stitches as
they face you, remembering to
always knit the edge stitches
(page 133).

Sleeves

1. With #6 needles, cast on 80 sts in
   color A. Work in pattern stitch for
   1", following striping sequence. At
   the same time, inc 1 st at each end
   EOR 2 times [84 sts; 15" wide and
   1" long].

2. Beg sleeve-cap shaping:
   - Bind off 3 sts at beg of next
     2 rows.
   - Bind off 2 sts at beg of next
     28 rows.
   - Dec 1 st at beg of next 10 rows.
   - Bind off last 12 sts.

Finishing

1. Because this is a ribbed sweater,
   steam each piece to size before
   sewing the garment together.
   "Opening up" the pieces will help
   ensure a better fit and make it
   easier to sew the pieces together.

2. Sew shoulder seams.

3. Front and neckband: With RS
   facing and #5 circular needle, pick
   up a total of 240 (248, 256) sts in
   color A:
   - 98 (102, 106) sts from lower left
     front to shoulder seam
   - 44 sts across back neck from
     shoulder to shoulder
   - 98 (102, 106) sts from shoulder
     seam to lower right front

   - Work 5 rows (changing color in
     sequence every row) in K2, P2
     rib. On buttonhole side, work 5
     buttonholes on 3rd row of rib,
     spacing them evenly between
     bottom and 1st neck dec. Bind
     off in pattern on 6th row.

4. Sew in sleeve caps; sew side and
   sleeve seams.

5. Sew on buttons to correspond with
   buttonholes.

6. Block assembled sweater to
   desired measurements.

7. Stabilize back neck and shoulders.

SLEEVE

BO 12

DEC 1 ST at BEG of next 10 rows.

BO 2 STS at BEG of next 28 rows.

7"

8"

BO 3   BO 3

15¾"
84 STS

INC 1 ST at each end EOR 2 times.

1"

15"

#6   CO 80 STS. Work in pattern.

RIBBED STRIPED CARDIGAN

Our second version of the ribbed cardigan came about because we purchased a beautiful 100 percent silk yarn that was only produced in four colors and had no "give" or memory. We wanted to show all the colors in one sweater, which the striping does effectively. The allover rib stitch gives the sweater the memory and movement that the yarn by itself does not have. The pattern is the same as the dressier first version, but the choice of yarn and longer length give it a more casual look. Please note with both sweaters how important the choice of buttons is in making each sweater unique—this is a great way to express your personal style!

Size

Small (Medium, Large)
Finished Bust: 32" (36", 40")
Finished Length: 18" (19", 20")

Materials

*Use the yarn listed in the chart or a
yarn that knits at 5.5 sts to 1". You
should have a total of 750
(850, 950) yds.*
#6 and #7 needles
#6 circular needle (40")
5 buttons

Gauge

22 sts and 26 rows = 4" in pattern
stitch using #7 needles
Always check gauge before starting
sweater. Increase or decrease
needle size to obtain correct gauge.

Skeins	Yards	Yarn	Color
3 (3, 4)	310 (360, 410)	Adrienne Vittadini Sabrina	A brown
2 (2, 3)	190 (240, 280)	Adrienne Vittadini Sabrina	B taupe
1	120	Adrienne Vittadini Sabrina	C turquoise
1	120	Adrienne Vittadini Sabrina	D ivory

Striping Sequence

No. of Rows	Color
6	A
4	B
2	C
4	D

Pattern Stitch

Multiple of 4, plus 2 edge stitches:
Row 1 (WS): K1, *K2, P2, rep from *,
end K1.
On remaining rows, work stitches as
they face you, remembering to always
knit the edge stitches (page 133).

*Note: Because ribbing naturally pulls in,
you will need to spread your piece a bit;
it should "open up" easily and not look
distorted to achieve the desired width
measurement.*

Back

1. With #6 needles, cast on 90 (102, 110) sts. Work in pattern stitch for 1", following striping sequence.

2. Switch to #7 needles and cont in pattern stitch until work measures 8½" (9½", 10½") from bottom [16" (18", 20") wide].

3. Beg armhole shaping:
   - Bind off 4 sts at beg of next 2 rows.
   - Dec 1 st at beg of next 8 rows [74 (84, 94) sts; 13" (15", 17") wide].

4. Cont until work measures 17" (18", 19") from bottom.

5. Beg back neck and shoulder shaping:
   - Bind off 6 (8, 10) sts. Work 14 (17, 20) sts. Keeping 15 (18, 21) sts on right-hand needle, bind off center 32 (34, 32) sts. Finish row. Turn work.
   - Bind off first 6 (8, 10) sts. Finish row. Turn work.
   - Dec 1 st at neck edge. Finish row. Turn work.

- Bind off 7 (8, 10) sts. Finish row. Turn work.
- Work across row. Turn work.
- Bind off last 7 (9, 10) sts.

6. Complete back neck and shoulder shaping:
   - Join yarn at neck edge. Dec 1 st and finish row. Turn work.
   - Bind off 7 (8, 10) sts. Finish row. Turn work.
   - Work across row. Turn work.
   - Bind off last 7 (9, 10) sts.

BACK

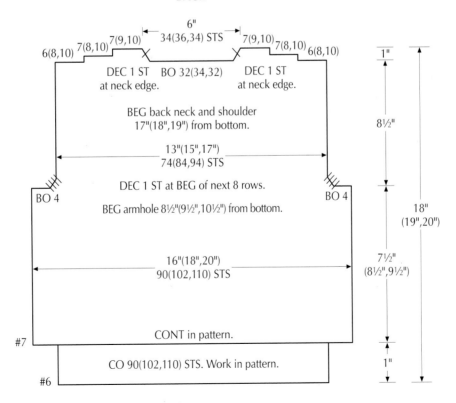

Fronts

1. With #6 needles, cast on 46 (50, 54) sts. Work in pattern stitch for 1", following striping sequence.

2. Switch to #7 needles and cont in pattern stitch until work measures $8^1/2$" ($9^1/2$", $10^1/2$") from bottom [8" (9", 10") wide].

3. Beg armhole shaping:
   - Bind off 4 sts at outside edge.
   - Dec 1 st at outside edge EOR 4 times [38 (42, 46) sts].

4. Cont in pattern until work measures 11" (12", 13") from bottom.

5. Beg neck shaping:
   - Dec 1 st at neck edge EOR 16 (17, 18) times.

6. Cont in pattern until work measures 17" (18", 19") from bottom.

7. Beg shoulder shaping:
   - Beg at outside edge, bind off first 6 (8, 10) sts. Finish row. Turn work.

   - Work across row. Turn work.
   - Bind off first 7 (8, 10) sts. Finish row. Turn work.
   - Work across row. Turn work.
   - Bind off last 7 (9, 10) sts.

8. Work second front the same as first front, but reverse the shaping.

FRONT

6(8,10) 7(8,10) 7(9,10)

DEC 1 ST at neck edge EOR 16(17,18) times.

BEG shoulder 17"(18",19") from bottom.

7"

BEG front neck 11"(12",13") from bottom.

7"(7½",8") 38(42,46) STS

DEC 1 ST at outside edge EOR 4 times.

BO 4

BEG armhole 8½"(9½",10½") from bottom.

8"(9",10") 46(50,54) STS

CONT in pattern.

#7

CO 46(50,54) STS. Work in pattern.

#6

1"

8½"

18" (19",20")

7½" (8½",9½")

1"

Sleeves

1. With #7 needles, cast on 80 sts in color A. Work in pattern stitch for 1", following striping sequence. At the same time, inc 1 st at each end EOR 2 times [84 sts; 15" wide and 1" long].
2. Beg sleeve-cap shaping:
   - Bind off 3 sts at beg of next 2 rows.
   - Bind off 2 sts at beg of next 28 rows.
   - Dec 1 st at beg of next 10 rows.
   - Bind off last 12 sts.

Finishing

1. Because this is a ribbed sweater, steam each piece to size before sewing the garment together. "Opening up" the pieces will help ensure a better fit and make it easier to sew the pieces together.
2. Sew shoulder seams.
3. Front and neckband: With RS facing and #6 circular needle, pick up a total of 201 (221, 241) sts in color A:
   - 79 (89, 99) sts from lower left front to shoulder seam
   - 43 sts across back neck from shoulder to shoulder
   - 79 (89, 99) sts from shoulder seam to lower right front
   - Work 5 rows in pattern stitch (changing color in sequence every row). On buttonhole side, work 5 buttonholes on 3rd row of rib, spacing them evenly between bottom edge and 1st neck dec. Bind off in pattern on 6th row.
4. Sew in sleeve caps; sew side and sleeve seams.
5. Sew on buttons to correspond with buttonholes.
6. Block assembled sweater to desired measurements.
7. Stabilize back neck and shoulders.

SLEEVE

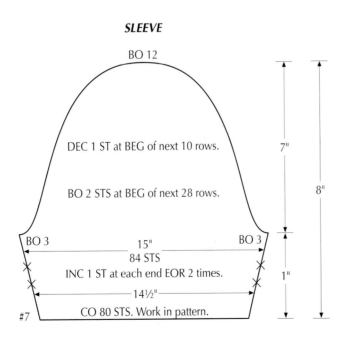

BO 12

DEC 1 ST at BEG of next 10 rows.

BO 2 STS at BEG of next 28 rows.

7"

8"

BO 3   15"   BO 3
            84 STS
INC 1 ST at each end EOR 2 times.
           14½"   1"
#7   CO 80 STS. Work in pattern.

All-Time
Favorite Jacket

GARTER STITCH JACKET

This is a perfect example of a yarn becoming the inspiration for a sweater. At our semiannual market, we discovered two incredible yarns. Both came from a multitalented Englishwoman named Colinette, who hand dyes beautiful fibers, ten skeins at a time, in old bathtubs.

We loved her palette, drawn from colors in nature. Not sure what we wanted to create, we begged for several skeins so we could knit swatches on the flight home. We came up with the shape you see here, but with only two skeins of each of the yarns, we knew we had to share the project.

To keep the gauge consistent as we each worked on separate pieces, one of us knit on #10½ and the other on #10¾ needles. If we'd both used the same-size needles, one front would have been several inches larger than the other!

When the yarn to complete the sweater arrived a month later, both of us were busy with new projects. Our colleague, Rose, completed the sleeves and collar. We laugh when customers tell us that it isn't really their sweater unless they knit every stitch. Many of ours would still be half finished if we didn't share the knitting!

This classic sweater has been our all-time best seller. We have sold literally hundreds over the past four years. It looks good on a wide variety of body types and sizes with only minor adjustments.

Size

Small (Medium, Large)
Finished Bust: 44" (49", 52")
Finished Length: 20" (22", 24")

Materials

Use 2 complementary yarns that knit at 2.55 sts to 1".

3 (4, 4) skeins of Colinette Fandango, each approximately 110 yds. (yarn A)

3 (4, 4) skeins of Colinette Zanziba, each approximately 103 yds. (yarn B) [600 (700, 800) yds. total]

#10½, #10¾, and #11 needles
#10½ circular needle (20")
Size J crochet hook
4 buttons

Striping Sequence

Alternate yarns A and B every 2 rows.

Gauge

10 sts and 17 rows = 4" in garter st using #10¾ needles
Always check gauge before starting sweater. Increase or decrease needle size to obtain correct gauge.

Back

1. With #11 needles, cast on 50 (56, 60) sts in yarn A.
2. Switch immediately to #10½ needles and knit 1 row in yarn A.

Note: We suggest casting on to a larger needle, then switching to a smaller one to knit bands because the yarn we chose has no give or elasticity. This ensures that the cast-on row is not too tight.

3. Knit 2 rows in yarn B.
4. Switch to #10¾ needles and cont in garter st, alternating 2 rows in yarn A and 2 rows in yarn B.

Note: When alternating yarns every two rows, it is not necessary to cut the yarn each time you change. Simply run them up the side until you get to the neck and shoulder shaping. This will reduce the number of ends to weave in later and creates a cleaner selvage edge.

5. At 2" from bottom of work, begin increases:
   ◆ Inc 1 st at each end every 2", 3 times [56 (62, 66) sts; 22" (24½", 26") wide].

BACK

Note: With this combination of yarns, CO to a #11 needle, then switch immediately to #10½ to complete ribbing. This will give you a looser cast-on row since Fandango has *no* give.

6. At 8½" (9½", 10½") from bottom of work, begin armhole shaping:
   - Bind off 2 sts at beg of next 2 rows.
   - Dec 1 st at beg of next 6 rows [46 (52, 56) sts; 18" (20", 22") wide].
7. Cont in garter st until work measures 18½" (20½", 22½") from bottom.
8. Beg back neck and shoulder shaping:
   - Bind off first 4 (5, 6) sts. Knit next 9 (11, 12) sts. Keeping 10 (12, 13) sts on the right-hand needle, bind off center 18 sts. Finish row. Turn work.
   - Bind off 4 (5, 6) sts. Finish row. Turn work.
   - Dec 1 st at neck edge. Finish row. Turn work.
   - Bind off 4 (5, 6) sts. Finish row. Turn work.
   - Knit across row. Turn work.
   - Bind off last 5 (6, 6) sts.
9. Complete neck and shoulder shaping:
   - Join yarn at neck edge. Dec 1 st and finish row. Turn work.
   - Bind off 4 (5, 6) sts. Finish row. Turn work.
   - Knit across row. Turn work.
   - Bind off last 5 (6, 6) sts.

Fronts

1. With #11 needles, cast on 25 (28, 30) sts in yarn A.
2. Switch immediately to #10½ needles and knit 1 row in yarn A.
3. Knit 2 rows in yarn B.
4. Switch to #10¾ needles and cont in garter st, alternating 2 rows in yarn A and 2 rows in yarn B.
5. At 2" from bottom of work, begin increases:
   - Inc 1 st at outside edge every 2" 3 times [28 (31, 33) sts; 11" (12", 13") wide].
6. At 8½" (9½", 10½") from bottom of work, beg armhole shaping:
   - Bind off 2 sts at outside edge.
   - Dec 1 st at outside edge EOR 3 times [23 (26, 28) sts; 9" (10", 11") wide].
7. Cont in garter st until work measures 16" (18", 20") from bottom.
8. Beg front neck shaping:
   - Beg at neck edge, bind off first 5 sts. Finish row. Turn work.
   - Work across row. Turn work.
   - Bind off 2 sts at neck edge. Finish row. Turn work.
   - Work across row. Turn work.

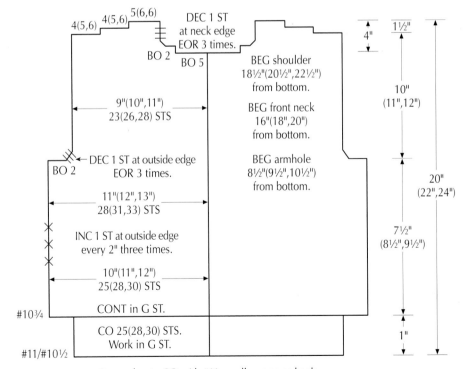

FRONT

4(5,6)   4(5,6)   5(6,6)   DEC 1 ST at neck edge EOR 3 times.

BO 2   BO 5   BEG shoulder 18½"(20½",22½") from bottom.

9"(10",11") 23(26,28) STS

BEG front neck 16"(18",20") from bottom.

DEC 1 ST at outside edge EOR 3 times.

BO 2

BEG armhole 8½"(9½",10½") from bottom.

11"(12",13") 28(31,33) STS

INC 1 ST at outside edge every 2" three times.

10"(11",12") 25(28,30) STS

CONT in G ST.

#10¾

CO 25(28,30) STS. Work in G ST.

#11/#10½

1½"   4"   10" (11",12")   20" (22",24")   7½" (8½",9½")   1"

Remember to CO with #11 needle, same as back.

◆ Dec 1 st at neck edge EOR 3 times.

9. Cont in garter st until work measures 18½" (20½", 22½") from bottom.

10. Beg shoulder shaping:
  ◆ Starting at outside edge, bind off first 4 (5, 6) sts. Finish row. Turn work.
  ◆ Work across row. Turn work.
  ◆ Bind off 4 (5, 6) sts. Finish row. Turn work.
  ◆ Work across row. Turn work.
  ◆ Bind off last 5 (6, 6) sts.

11. Work second front the same as first, but reverse the shaping.

Sleeves

1. With #11 needles, cast on 24 sts in yarn A.

2. Switch immediately to #10½ needles and knit 1 row in yarn A.

3. Work in garter st with yarn B for 2 rows.

4. Switch to #10¾ needles. Cont in garter st; inc 1 st at each end every 4 rows 12 (15, 18) times [48 (54, 60) sts; 19" (21", 23") wide].

5. Cont in garter st until work measures 15" (16", 17") from bottom.

6. Beg sleeve-cap shaping:
  ◆ Bind off 4 (6, 6) sts at beg of next 2 rows.
  ◆ Bind off 5 (6, 6) sts at beg of next 2 rows.
  ◆ Bind off 5 (5, 6) sts at beg of next 2 rows.
  ◆ Bind off 5 (5, 7) sts at beg of next 2 rows.
  ◆ Bind off last 10 sts.

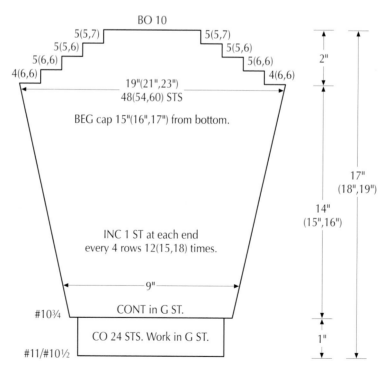

SLEEVE

BO 10

5(5,7) 5(5,7)
5(5,6) 5(5,6)
5(6,6) 5(6,6)
4(6,6) 4(6,6)

19"(21",23")
48(54,60) STS

BEG cap 15"(16",17") from bottom.

2"

17" (18",19")

14" (15",16")

INC 1 ST at each end every 4 rows 12(15,18) times.

9"

CONT in G ST.

#10¾

CO 24 STS. Work in G ST.

#11/#10½

1"

Note: Remember to CO with #11 needle, same as back.

Finishing

1. Sew shoulder seams.
2. Collar: With RS facing and #10$^1/_2$ circular needle, pick up a total of 58 sts:
   - 17 sts from center front to shoulder seam
   - 24 sts from shoulder seam to shoulder seam
   - 17 sts from shoulder seam to center front

- Work in garter st for 1".
- Inc 5 sts evenly in the next row (but not at the beginning or end of row). Create increases using the Make One technique (page 134) [63 sts].
- Work in garter st for 1".
- Inc 5 more sts evenly, as before, lining them up with the previous increases [68 sts].
- Cont until collar measures 3$^1/_2$".
- Bind off loosely.

3. Sew in sleeve caps; sew side and sleeve seams.
4. Work 2 rows of single crochet in yarn B on both fronts, placing buttonholes in 2nd row as desired.
5. Sew on buttons to correspond with buttonholes.
6. Block assembled sweater to desired measurements.
7. Stabilize back neck and shoulders.

Classic Cardigans
TRADITIONAL SUMMER CARDIGAN

Some sweater shapes are classic and timeless because they work with everything and make you feel good every time you slip them on. We have made this sweater with intricate color-work bands and multicolor pattern work in the body; in cotton solids for summer; and in wool, mohair, and even cashmere for winter. We have striped it, tweeded two colors together, and knit it in stockinette stitch and a variety of pattern stitches.

We have some customers who like to wear this shape longer over leggings, others who like it short, to wear with skirts or slacks. This is a sweater that, once you find your particular favorite dimensions, you will knit several times using different yarns.

This sweater was knit with two Missoni yarns run together and treated as one. Striped bands repeat all of the colors in the variegated yarn that runs throughout the body of the sweater.

Size

Small (Medium, Large)
Finished Bust: 40" (44", 48")
Finished Length: 27$\frac{1}{2}$" (28$\frac{1}{2}$", 29$\frac{1}{2}$")

Materials

*Use a combination of yarns that knit
at 3.5 sts to 1".*

◆ Body of sweater (two yarns run
together):
8 (9, 10) skeins of Missoni Kos,
each approximately 116 yds. [925
(1050, 1150) yds. total]
8 (9, 10) skeins of Missoni Lima,
each approximately 115 yds. [925
(1050, 1150) yds. total]
◆ Color bands:
1 skein each of 6 colors of
Missoni Caprera or sport yarn,
each approximately 120 yds.

#3 circular needle (40" to 47")
#3 double-pointed needles
#9 needles
4 stitch holders
6 buttons

Band Striping Sequence

Row	Yarn	Color
Rows 1, 3, 5, 7, 9, 11, 13, 15, and 17 of bands	Missoni Kos	A #252
Rows 2 and 14 of bands	Missoni Caprera	B rust
Rows 4 and 16 of bands	Missoni Caprera	C teal
Rows 6 and 18 of bands	Missoni Caprera	D burgundy
Row 8 of bands	Missoni Caprera	E sienna
Row 10 of bands	Missoni Caprera	F purple
Row 12 of bands	Missoni Caprera	G yellow

Body of sweater

Row	Yarn	Color
A and H run together	Missoni Kos	A #252
	Missoni Lima	H #505

Gauge

14 sts and 20 rows = 4" in St st using
#9 needles with yarn doubled
Always check gauge before starting
sweater. Increase or decrease
needle size to obtain correct gauge.

*Note: All ribbings are worked back and
forth in rows on a circular needle.
Because only one row is worked in each
color, it will not be necessary to turn your
work at the end of every row. Slide
stitches to beginning or end of needle as
needed to pick up the next color.*

Back

Note: Because the bands are knit using a much smaller yarn than the body, you will notice that we decrease quite a few stitches (and increase needle sizes) when we transition from the bands to the body of the sweater.

1. With #3 circular needle, cast on 116 (122, 128) sts using color A. Work in K1, P1 rib for 2½", following band striping sequence.

2. Switch to #9 needles. Working in St st, with yarns A and H run together, dec 44 sts evenly across first row of body [72 (78, 84) sts; 20" (22", 24") wide].

3. Cont in St st until work measures 17½" (18", 18½") from bottom.

4. Beg armhole shaping:
   - ◆ Bind off 3 sts at beg of next 2 rows.
   - ◆ Dec 1 st at beg of next 4 rows [62 (68, 74) sts; 17" (19", 21") wide].

5. Cont until work measures 26½" (27½", 28½") from bottom.

6. Beg back neck and shoulder shaping:
   - ◆ Bind off first 6 (7, 8) sts. Knit next 13 (15, 17) sts. Keeping 14 (16, 18) sts on right-hand needle, bind off center 22 sts. Finish row. Turn work.

- ◆ Bind off 6 (7, 8) sts. Finish row. Turn work.
- ◆ Dec 1 st at neck edge. Finish row. Turn work.
- ◆ Bind off 6 (7, 8) sts. Finish row. Turn work.
- ◆ Knit across row. Turn work.
- ◆ Bind off last 7 (8, 9) sts.

7. Complete back neck and shoulder shaping:
   - ◆ Join yarn at neck edge. Dec 1 st and finish row. Turn work.
   - ◆ Bind off 6 (7, 8) sts. Finish row. Turn work.
   - ◆ Purl across row. Turn work.
   - ◆ Bind off last 7 (8, 9) sts.

BACK

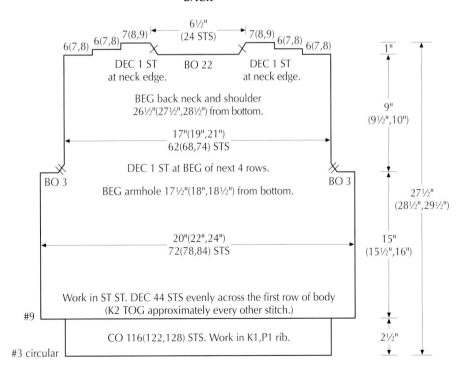

6½"
(24 STS)

6(7,8) 6(7,8) 7(8,9) 7(8,9) 6(7,8) 6(7,8)

DEC 1 ST at neck edge.   BO 22   DEC 1 ST at neck edge.

BEG back neck and shoulder 26½"(27½",28½") from bottom.

1"

17"(19",21")
62(68,74) STS

9"
(9½",10")

DEC 1 ST at BEG of next 4 rows.

BO 3   BEG armhole 17½"(18",18½") from bottom.   BO 3

27½"
(28½",29½")

20"(22",24")
72(78,84) STS

15"
(15½",16")

Work in ST ST. DEC 44 STS evenly across the first row of body (K2 TOG approximately every other stitch.)

#9

CO 116(122,128) STS. Work in K1,P1 rib.

2½"

#3 circular

Fronts

1. Knit 2 pocket linings:
   - With #9 needles, cast on 18 sts using A and H run together. Work in St st for 4". Put work on stitch holders and set aside.

2. Begin with left front. With #3 circular needles, cast on 58 (61, 64) sts using color A. Work in K1, P1 rib for 2 1/2", following band striping sequence.

3. Switch to #9 needles. Working in St st, with yarns A and H run together, dec 22 sts evenly across first row of body [36 (39, 42) sts; 10" (11", 12") wide].

4. Cont in St st until work measures 7 1/2" from bottom.

5. Work left front pocket, starting at side seam:
   - Knit first 9 (11, 12) sts. Place next 18 sts on a stitch holder.
   - Knit 18 sts of first pocket lining off the stitch holder.
   - Knit last 9 (10, 12) sts.

6. Cont until work measures 14 1/2" (15 1/2", 16 1/2") from bottom.

7. Beg neck shaping:
   - Dec 1 st at neck edge every 6 rows 6 times.
   - Dec 1 st at neck edge every 4 rows 6 times.

Remember to measure the length of your work frequently, since you will need to begin armhole shaping shortly.

8. When work measures 17 1/2" (18", 18 1/2") from bottom, beg armhole shaping:
   - Bind off 3 sts at outside edge of next row. Finish row. Turn work.
   - Work across row. Turn work.
   - Dec 1 st at outside edge EOR 2 times.

9. Cont until work measures 26 1/2" (27 1/2", 28 1/2") from bottom.

10. Complete shoulder shaping:
    - Beg at outside edge, bind off first 6 (7, 8) sts. Finish row. Turn work.
    - Work across row. Turn work.
    - Bind off 6 (7, 8) sts. Finish row. Turn work.
    - Work across row. Turn work.
    - Bind off last 7 (8, 9) sts.

11. Work right front the same as left front, but reverse the shaping.

12. Work right front pocket, starting at center front:
    - Knit first 9 (10, 12) sts. Place next 18 sts on a stitch holder.
    - Knit 18 sts of pocket lining off the stitch holder.
    - Knit last 9 (11, 12) sts.

FRONT

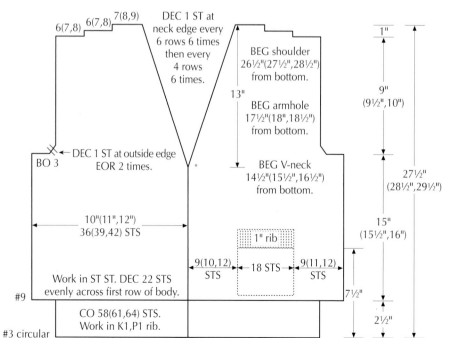

6(7,8) 6(7,8) 7(8,9)

DEC 1 ST at neck edge every 6 rows 6 times then every 4 rows 6 times.

BEG shoulder 26 1/2"(27 1/2",28 1/2") from bottom.

BEG armhole 17 1/2"(18",18 1/2") from bottom.

13"

1"

9" (9 1/2",10")

DEC 1 ST at outside edge EOR 2 times.

BO 3

BEG V-neck 14 1/2"(15 1/2",16 1/2") from bottom.

27 1/2" (28 1/2",29 1/2")

10"(11",12") 36(39,42) STS

1" rib

15" (15 1/2",16")

Work in ST ST. DEC 22 STS evenly across first row of body.

9(10,12) STS   18 STS   9(11,12) STS

7 1/2"

#9

CO 58(61,64) STS. Work in K1,P1 rib.

2 1/2"

#3 circular

Sleeves

1. With #3 circular needle, cast on 50 (52, 54) sts using color A. Work in K1, P1 rib for $2^1/2$", following band striping sequence.

2. Switch to #9 needles. Working in St st, with yarns A and H run together, dec 14 sts evenly across first row of sleeve [36 (38, 40) sts; $10^1/2$" (11", $11^1/2$") wide].

3. Work 1" in St st; inc 1 st at each end every 6 rows 10 (11, 12) times [56 (60, 64) sts; 16" (17", 18") wide].

4. Cont until work measures 15" (17", 19") from bottom.

5. Beg sleeve-cap shaping:
   ◆ Bind off 3 sts at beg of next 6 rows.
   ◆ Bind off 3 (3, 4) sts at beg of next 4 rows.
   ◆ Bind off 3 (4, 4) sts at beg of next 4 rows.
   ◆ Bind off last 14 sts.

Finishing

1. Sew shoulder seams.

2. Complete the pockets:
   ◆ Slip the sts off the stitch holder onto #3 double-pointed needles. Work K1, P1 rib in yarn A; inc 4 sts evenly across row.
   ◆ Work through 1 stripe sequence in K1, P1 rib.
   ◆ Bind off in rib pattern.
   ◆ Slipstitch the pocket lining and edges of the ribbing in place.

3. Front bands: With RS facing and #3 circular needle, pick up a total of 345 (357, 369) sts in yarn A:
   ◆ 156 (162, 168) sts from lower right front to shoulder seam
   ◆ 33 sts from shoulder seam to shoulder seam
   ◆ 156 (162, 168) sts from shoulder seam to lower left front
   ◆ Work in K1, P1 rib for $1^1/4$", following striping sequence. On buttonhole side, work 6 buttonholes in 4th row of rib, spacing them evenly between the bottom and first neck decrease. Bind off in pattern.

4. Sew in sleeve caps; sew side and sleeve seams.

5. Sew on buttons to correspond with buttonholes.

6. Block assembled sweater to desired measurements.

7. Stabilize back neck and shoulders.

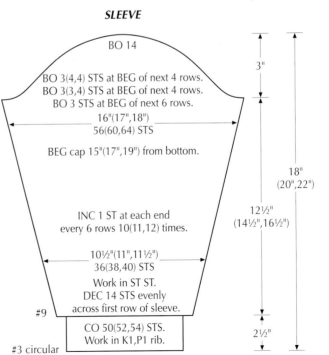

SLEEVE

BO 14

BO 3(4,4) STS at BEG of next 4 rows.
BO 3(3,4) STS at BEG of next 4 rows.
BO 3 STS at BEG of next 6 rows.

16"(17",18")
56(60,64) STS

BEG cap 15"(17",19") from bottom.

3"

18"
(20",22")

$12^1/2$"
($14^1/2$",$16^1/2$")

INC 1 ST at each end every 6 rows 10(11,12) times.

$10^1/2$"(11",$11^1/2$")
36(38,40) STS
Work in ST ST.
DEC 14 STS evenly across first row of sleeve.

#9

CO 50(52,54) STS.
Work in K1,P1 rib.

$2^1/2$"

#3 circular

STRIPED CARDIGAN

This is an example of how great color and texture combinations can transform the simplest shape into a truly exciting sweater! We combined two multicolor textured yarns for the base, then set off the striping with solid colors to intensify and "pop" the colors.

Every time we repeat this particular shape, it becomes a new favorite. We vary the bands to further change the look, but the basic dimensions (other than the length) change little.

Size

Small (Medium, Large)

Finished Bust: 44" (48", 52")

Finished Length: 28$\frac{1}{2}$" (29$\frac{1}{2}$", 30$\frac{1}{2}$")

Materials

Use Filatura di Crosa Oxford, doubled,
in the colors listed in the chart or a
yarn that knits at 3.8 sts to 1":

#7 and #8 needles

#6 circular needle (47")

Stitch holder

5 (5, 6) buttons

Gauge

15 sts and 21 rows = 4" in St st using
#8 needles

Always check gauge before starting
sweater. Increase or decrease
needle size to obtain correct gauge.

Rib Striping Sequence

1 row of each color with yarn
doubled:

A white

B green

C blue

D yellow

E dk. green

F orange

G rust

Skeins	Yards	Color
6 (6, 7)	950 (1000, 1050)	A #351 white
2 (2, 3)	300 (320, 340)	B #352 green
2 (2, 3)	300 (320, 340)	C #354 blue
2 (2, 3)	300 (320, 340)	D #356 yellow
4 (4, 5)	600 (650, 700)	E #357 dk. green
2 (2, 3)	300 (320, 340)	F #350 orange
2 (2, 3)	300 (320, 340)	G #353 rust

Body Striping Sequence

(with yarn doubled)

No. of Rows	Color	No. of Rows	Color
3	A white	3	A white
7	B green	7	F orange
3	A white	3	A white
5	E dk. green	5	B green
3	A white	3	A white
3	E dk. green	5	E dk. green
3	A white	3	A white
3	E dk. green	3	E dk. green
3	A white	3	A white
7	D yellow	5	G rust
3	A white	3	A white
7	G rust	7	D yellow
3	A white	3	A white
5	B green	5	B green
3	A white	3	A white
3	E dk. green	3	E dk. green
3	A white	3	A white
5	C blue	3	E dk. green

Back

1. With #7 needles, cast on 86 (94, 100) sts using color A doubled. Work in K1, P1 rib for 2$^1/_2$", following rib striping sequence and ending with 1 row of color G.

2. Switch to #8 needles and work in St st, following body striping sequence.

3. Cont until work measures 18" (18$^1/_2$", 19") from bottom [22" (24", 26") wide].

4. Beg armhole shaping:
   ◆ Bind off 2 sts at beg of next 6 rows.

   ◆ Dec 1 st at beg of next 4 rows [70 (78, 84) sts; 18" (20", 22") wide].

5. Cont until work measures 27$^1/_2$" (28$^1/_2$", 29$^1/_2$") from bottom.

6. Beg back neck and shoulder shaping:
   ◆ Bind off first 7 (8, 9) sts. Knit next 15 (17, 20) sts. Keeping 16 (18, 21) sts on right-hand needle, bind off center 24 sts. Finish row. Turn work.
   ◆ Bind off first 7 (8, 9) sts. Finish row. Turn work.
   ◆ Dec 1 st at neck edge. Finish row. Turn work.

   ◆ Bind off 7 (8, 10) sts. Finish row. Turn work.
   ◆ Work across row. Turn work.
   ◆ Bind off last 8 (9, 10) sts.

7. Complete back neck and shoulder shaping:
   ◆ Join yarn at neck edge. Dec 1 st and finish row. Turn work.
   ◆ Bind off 7 (8, 10) sts. Finish row. Turn work.
   ◆ Work across row. Turn work.
   ◆ Bind off last 8 (9, 10) sts.

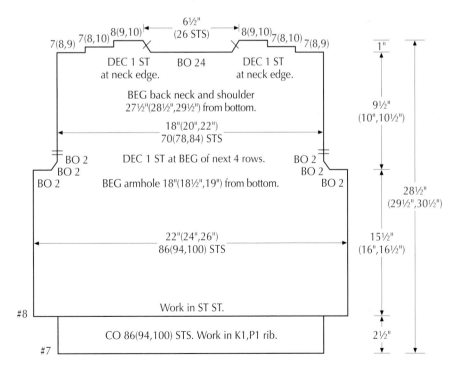

BACK

Fronts

1. Knit 2 pocket linings:
   - With #7 needles, cast on 20 (20, 21) sts using color A doubled.
   - Work in St st in body striping sequence until work measures 5". Bind off and set aside.
2. Begin with left front. With #7 needles, cast on 42 (45, 49) sts using color A doubled. Work in K1, P1 rib for 2 1/2", following rib striping sequence and ending with 1 row of color G.
3. Switch to #8 needles and work in St st, following body striping sequence [11" (12", 13") wide].
4. Cont in St st until work measures 7 1/2" from bottom.
5. Work left front pocket, starting at side seam.
   - Knit the first 11 (12, 14) sts. Place the center 20 (20, 21) sts on a stitch holder.
   - Knit the 20 (20, 21) sts of the first pocket lining off the stitch holder.
   - Knit the last 11 (13, 14) sts.
6. Cont until work measures 15 1/2" (16 1/2", 17 1/2") from bottom.
7. Beg V-neck shaping:
   - Dec 1 st at neck edge every 6 rows 12 times.
8. At 18" (18 1/2", 19") from bottom, beg armhole shaping (while continuing neck decreases):
   - Bind off 2 sts at outside edge EOR 3 times.
   - Dec 1 st at outside edge EOR 2 times.
9. Cont in St st, working V-neck shaping, until work measures 27 1/2" (28 1/2", 29 1/2") from bottom.
10. Complete shoulder shaping:
    - Beg at outside edge, bind off first 7 (8, 9) sts. Finish row. Turn work.
    - Work across row. Turn work.
    - Bind off 7 (8, 10) sts. Finish row. Turn work.
    - Work across row. Turn work.
    - Bind off last 8 (9, 10) sts.
11. Work right front the same as left front, but reverse the shaping.
12. Work right front pocket, starting at center front:
    - Knit first 11 (13, 14) sts. Place next 20 (20,21) sts on a stitch holder.
    - Knit 20 (20, 21) sts of pocket lining off the stitch holder.
    - Knit the last 11 (12, 14) sts.

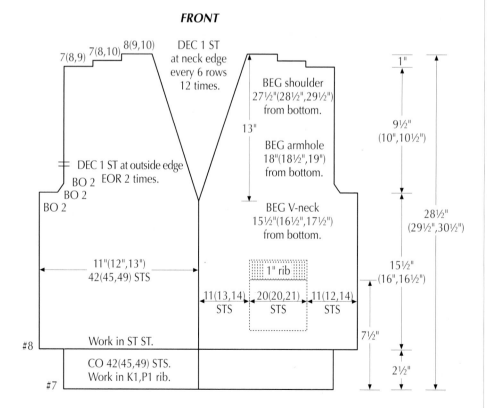

FRONT

7(8,9) 7(8,10) 8(9,10)

DEC 1 ST at neck edge every 6 rows 12 times.

BEG shoulder 27 1/2"(28 1/2",29 1/2") from bottom.

1"

DEC 1 ST at outside edge EOR 2 times.
BO 2
BO 2
BO 2

13"

BEG armhole 18"(18 1/2",19") from bottom.

9 1/2" (10",10 1/2")

BEG V-neck 15 1/2"(16 1/2",17 1/2") from bottom.

28 1/2" (29 1/2",30 1/2")

11"(12",13") 42(45,49) STS

1" rib

11(13,14) STS   20(20,21) STS   11(12,14) STS

15 1/2" (16",16 1/2")

Work in ST ST.

7 1/2"

#8

CO 42(45,49) STS. Work in K1,P1 rib.

2 1/2"

#7

Sleeves

1. With #7 needles, cast on 34 (36, 38) sts using color A doubled. Work in K1, P1 rib for 2½", following rib striping sequence and ending with 1 row of color G.
   - ◆ Inc 4 sts in last row of rib [38 (40, 42) sts].
2. Switch to #8 needles and work in St st, following body striping sequence [10" (10½", 11") wide]. Inc 1 st at each end every 6 rows 15 times [68 (70, 72) sts; 18" (18½", 19") wide].
3. Cont until work measures 15½" (17", 18½") from bottom.
4. Work sleeve-cap shaping:
   - ◆ Bind off 2 sts at beg of next 6 rows.
   - ◆ Bind off 3 sts at beg of next 14 rows.
   - ◆ Bind off last 14 (16, 18) sts.

Finishing

1. Sew shoulder seams.
2. Front and neckbands: With RS facing and #6 circular needle, pick up a total of 259 (267, 275) sts using color A doubled:
   - ◆ 114 (118, 122) sts from lower right front to shoulder
   - ◆ 31 sts from shoulder to shoulder
   - ◆ 114 (118, 122) sts from shoulder to lower left front
   - ◆ Work in K1, P1 rib in single-row stripes for 1½". On buttonhole side, work 5 (5, 6) buttonholes in 4th row of rib, spacing them evenly between the bottom and first V-neck decrease. Bind off in pattern.
3. Complete pockets:
   - ◆ Slip the pocket stitches off the holder onto #7 needles and work 1" in K1, P1 rib, changing colors every row. Bind off in pattern.
   - ◆ Slipstitch pocket linings in place.
   - ◆ Slipstitch ribbing down at edges of pockets.
4. Sew in sleeve caps; sew side and sleeve seams.
5. Sew on buttons to correspond with buttonholes.
6. Block assembled sweater to desired measurements.
7. Stabilize back neck and shoulders.

SLEEVE

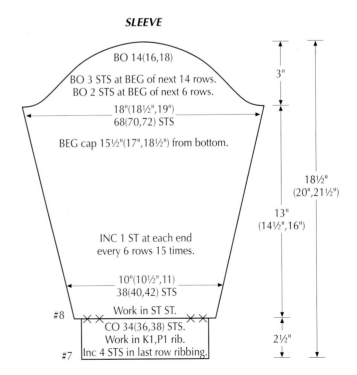

BO 14(16,18)

BO 3 STS at BEG of next 14 rows.
BO 2 STS at BEG of next 6 rows.

18"(18½",19")
68(70,72) STS

BEG cap 15½"(17",18½") from bottom.

3"

18½"
(20",21½")

13"
(14½",16")

INC 1 ST at each end
every 6 rows 15 times.

10"(10½",11)
38(40,42) STS

#8   Work in ST ST.
        CO 34(36,38) STS.
        Work in K1,P1 rib.
#7   Inc 4 STS in last row ribbing.

2½"

Spectacular Striping

MULTI-STRIPE PULLOVER

One of the hardest parts of being a yarnaholic is trying to remember that, as excited about all of the beautiful new yarns as we are at the beginning of a new season, new, even more spectacular yarns will arrive next season.

Often, like fashion, a particular yarn is only available for one season. After several seasons, we end up with a basket of beautiful, but seemingly useless odds and ends. This basket was actually the catalyst for the sweater you see here, and the striping was determined by the availability of the yarns. Sometimes it's worth it to throw in just a single, one-row stripe of an old favorite, just as you would a treasured scrap from one of your grandfather's old shirts or ties when making a quilt. These sweaters represent our knitting history!

We also don't have time to knit with every one of the gorgeous yarns that come in. This pullover lets us knit many of them in a single sweater.

Front

1. Knit 2 pocket linings:
   - With #6 needles, cast on 26 sts in yarn B.
   - Work in St st for 5". Put both pocket linings on stitch holders and set aside.
2. With #4 needles, cast on 108 (118, 128) sts in yarn B. Work in K1, P1 rib for 1½".
3. Switch to #6 needles. Work in St st, following striping sequence, until work measures 8" from bottom [21½" (23½", 25½") wide].
4. Work pockets:

- Knit first 18 (21, 25) sts; place next 26 sts on a holder.
- Knit 26 sts of first pocket lining off the stitch holder.
- Knit center 20 (24, 26) sts.
- Place next 26 sts on another stitch holder (this is your second pocket).
- Knit 26 sts of second pocket lining off the stitch holder.
- Knit last 18 (21, 25) sts.
5. Cont until work measures 16" (17½", 19") from bottom.
6. Beg armhole shaping:
   - Bind off 8 (8, 7) sts at beg of

next 2 rows [92 (102, 114) sts; 18" (20", 22") wide].
7. Cont until work measures 19" (21", 23") from bottom.
8. Beg V-neck shaping:
   - Work right front (the one you wear on your right side) first. Place first 46 (51, 57) sts on a stitch holder.
   - Dec 1 st at neck edge every 2 rows 18 times [28 (33, 39) sts].
9. Cont until work measures 25" (27", 29") from bottom.
10. Complete right shoulder shaping:
    - Starting at outside edge, bind off first 9 (11, 13) sts. Finish row. Turn work.
    - Work across row. Turn work.
    - Bind off 9 (11, 13) sts. Finish row. Turn work.
    - Work across row. Turn work.
    - Bind off last 10 (11, 13) sts.
11. Complete neck shaping on left half of front:
    - Slip the stitches from stitch holder back onto needle.
    - Join yarn at neck edge and complete shaping as for right front.
12. Cont until work measures 25" (27", 29") from bottom.
13. Work left shoulder the same as right shoulder, but reverse the shaping.

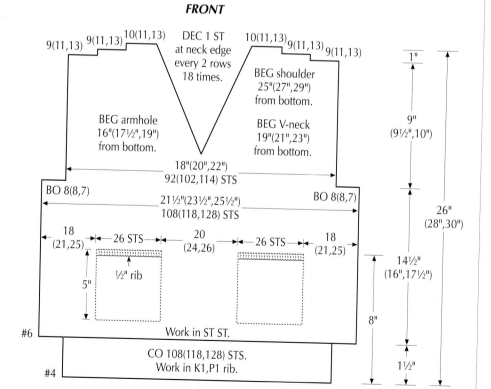

118

Sleeves

1. With #4 needles, cast on 58 (62, 66) sts with ribbing yarn. Work in K1, P1 rib for 1 1/2", following striping sequence.

2. Switch to #6 needles. Work in St st, following striping sequence, for 1".
   ◆ Inc 1 st at each end every 4 rows 14 (15, 15) times [86 (92, 96) sts; 17" (18", 19") wide].

3. Cont until work measures 12" from bottom.

4. Beg sleeve-cap shaping:
   ◆ Bind off 6 (7, 7) sts at beg of next 4 rows.
   ◆ Bind off 7 (7, 8) sts at beg of next 4 rows.
   ◆ Bind off 7 (8, 8) sts at beg of next 2 rows.
   ◆ Bind off last 20 sts.

Finishing

1. Complete pockets:
   ◆ Slip stitches off the holder onto #4 needles and work in K1, P1 rib for 1", following striping sequence. Bind off in pattern.
   ◆ Slipstitch pocket linings in place.
   ◆ Slipstitch ribbing down at edge of each pocket.

2. Sew shoulder seams.

3. Sew in sleeve caps; sew side and sleeve seams.

4. Work 1 row of single crochet around neck.

5. Block assembled sweater to desired measurements.

6. Stabilize back neck and shoulders.

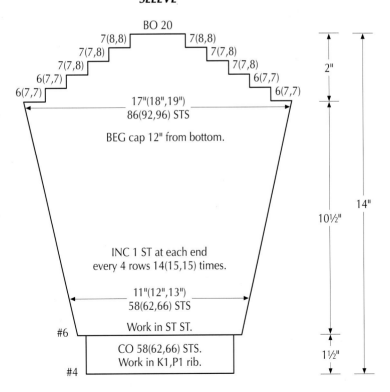

SLEEVE

BO 20

7(8,8)   7(8,8)

7(7,8)   7(7,8)

7(7,8)   7(7,8)

6(7,7)   6(7,7)

6(7,7)   6(7,7)

17"(18",19")
86(92,96) STS

BEG cap 12" from bottom.

2"

INC 1 ST at each end every 4 rows 14(15,15) times.

11"(12",13")
58(62,66) STS

Work in ST ST.

14"

10½"

#6

CO 58(62,66) STS.
Work in K1,P1 rib.

#4

1½"

MULTI-STRIPE CARDIGAN

For a dressier version of the multi-stripe sweater, we chose to add a metallic yarn in three complementary colors. It is used in two-color checks spaced throughout the body and sleeves. For added interest we have varied the striping pattern, with narrower stripes at the bottom and wider stripes across the chest and shoulders. When knitting stripes with a variety of yarns, there is often a fair amount of extra yarn left over after the sweater is complete. You might consider using your extras in a simple striped shell to wear under your cardigan.

Size

Small (Medium, Large)
Finished Bust: 43" (47", 51")
Finished Length: 26" (28", 30")

Materials

Use the yarns listed in the chart or 14 to 18 complementary yarns in a variety of textures that, when knit together in a random-stripe pattern, knit at approximately 5 sts to 1".

#3 and #6 needles
#3 circular needle (40" or 47")
4 stitch holders
6 buttons

Gauge

5.0 sts and 6.6 rows = 1" in St st using #6 needles
Always check gauge before starting sweater. Increase or decrease needle size to obtain correct gauge.

When running multiple strands of yarn together as one or when working with skeins that are very slippery and tend to unwind easily, it is helpful to seal the skein(s) in a zipper-lock bag and cut off one corner of the bag to run the strands through. This will save many hours of untangling.

TRICOTER Knitting specialists

Skeins	Yards*	Yarn	Color	
1 each	164	Filatura di Crosa No Smoking	D	#136 cobalt
	164	Filatura di Crosa No Smoking	H	#129 lt. blue
	164	Filatura di Crosa No Smoking	O	#112 gold
	110	Missoni Astra	L	#5 orange
	110	Missoni Astra	J	#13 black
	109	Missoni Atene	M	#908 raspberry
	109	Missoni Atene	K	#902 salmon
	121	Missoni Kos	N	#309 orange
	121	Missoni Kos	I	#314 blue
2 each	328	Filatura di Crosa No Smoking	D, H, O	#142 green
	184	Filatura di Crosa Kandalama	B	#201 lt. green
	184	Filatura di Crosa Kandalama	F	#204 dk. green
	292	Filatura di Crosa Malindi	C	#702 navy
	218	Missoni Atene	E	#900 green
	242	Missoni Kos	A	#320 green
	196	Missoni Camogli	G	#21 blue/green

*The number of yards is approximate.

Striping Sequence #1

(from bottom to armholes)

No. of Rows		Color	No. of Rows		Color
2	A	#320 green	2	I	#314 blue
2	B	#201 lt. green	2	J	#13 black
2	C	#702 navy	2	K	#902 salmon
2	D*	#142 green & #136 cobalt	2	L	#5 orange
2	E	#900 green	2	M	#908 raspberry
2	F	#204 dk. green	2	N	#309 orange
2	G	#21 blue/green	2	O*	#142 green & #112 gold
2	H*	#142 green & #129 lt. blue			

Repeat sequence.

* On these rows, work the 2 colors in a check pattern, alternating 3 sts of each color.

Striping Sequence #2

(from armholes to shoulders)

No. of

Rows	Color
5	A #320 green
5	B #201 lt. green
5	C #702 navy
2	D* #142 green & #136 cobalt
5	E #900 green
5	F #204 dk. green
5	G #21 blue/green
2	H* #142 green & #129 lt. blue
2	I #314 blue
2	J #13 black
2	K #902 salmon
2	L #5 orange
2	M #908 raspberry
2	N #309 orange
2	O* #142 green & #112 gold

Repeat sequence.

* On these rows, work the 2 colors in a check pattern, alternating 3 sts of each color.

Back

1. With #3 needles, cast on 108 (118, 128) sts. Work in K1, P1 rib for 1", following striping sequence #1.
2. Switch to #6 needles. Work in St st, following striping sequence, until work measures 15" (16½", 18") from bottom [21½" (23½", 25½") wide]. Change to striping sequence #2 at this point. (If you prefer, you may continue with the same striping for the remainder of the body, but the yarn amounts may vary.)
3. Work armhole shaping:
   - Bind off 8 (8, 7) sts at beg of next 2 rows [92 (102, 114) sts; 18" (20", 22") wide].
4. Cont until work measures 25" (27", 29") from bottom.
5. Beg back neck and shoulder shaping:
   - Bind off first 9 (11, 13) sts. Knit next 19 (22, 26) sts. Keeping 20 (23, 27) sts on right-hand needle, bind off center 34 sts. Finish row. Turn work.
   - Bind off 9 (11, 13) sts. Finish row. Turn work.
   - Dec 1 st at neck edge and finish row. Turn work.
   - Bind off 9 (11, 13) sts. Finish row. Turn work.
   - Knit across row. Turn work.
   - Bind off last 10 (11, 13) sts.
6. Complete back neck and shoulder shaping:
   - Join yarn at neck edge. Dec 1 st and finish row. Turn work.
   - Bind off 9 (11, 13) sts. Finish row. Turn work.
   - Purl across row. Turn work.
   - Bind off last 10 (11, 13) sts.

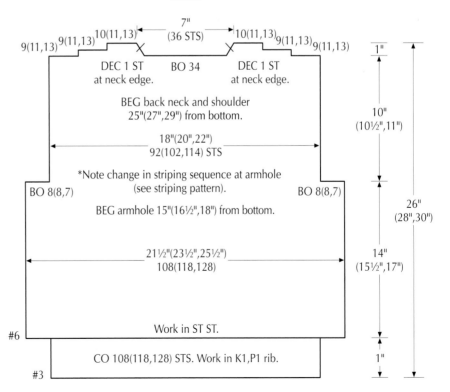

BACK

9(11,13) 9(11,13) 10(11,13) | 7" (36 STS) | 10(11,13) 9(11,13) 9(11,13)

DEC 1 ST at neck edge.   BO 34   DEC 1 ST at neck edge.

BEG back neck and shoulder 25"(27",29") from bottom.

18"(20",22") 92(102,114) STS

*Note change in striping sequence at armhole (see striping pattern).

BO 8(8,7)   BEG armhole 15"(16½",18") from bottom.   BO 8(8,7)

21½"(23½",25½") 108(118,128)

#6   Work in ST ST.

CO 108(118,128) STS. Work in K1,P1 rib.

#3

1"

10" (10½",11")

26" (28",30")

14" (15½",17")

1"

Fronts

1. With #3 needles, cast on 52 (56, 62) sts. Work in K1, P1 rib for 1", following striping sequence #1.

2. Switch to #6 needles. Work in St st, following striping sequence, until work measures 14" (15", 16") from bottom [10" (11", 12") wide].

3. Beg neck shaping:
   ♦ Dec 1 st at neck edge every 5 rows 16 times.

Note: Armhole shaping begins shortly after you begin neck shaping, so remember to measure.

4. Beg armhole shaping at 15" (16½", 18") from bottom, following striping sequence #2.
   ♦ Bind off 8 (7, 7) sts at beg of outside edge.

5. Cont until work measures 25" (27", 29") from bottom [28 (33, 39) sts].

6. Complete shoulder shaping:
   ♦ Bind off first 9 (11, 13) sts. Finish row. Turn work.
   ♦ Work across row. Turn work.
   ♦ Bind off 9 (11, 13) sts. Finish row. Turn work.
   ♦ Work across row. Turn work.
   ♦ Bind off last 10 (11, 13) sts.

7. Work second front the same as first front, but reverse the shaping.

FRONT

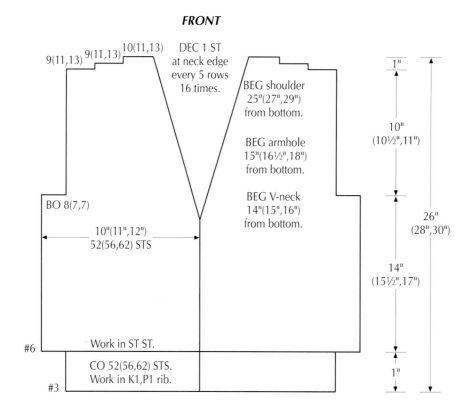

9(11,13) 9(11,13) 10(11,13)

DEC 1 ST at neck edge every 5 rows 16 times.

BEG shoulder 25"(27",29") from bottom.

BEG armhole 15"(16½",18") from bottom.

BEG V-neck 14"(15",16") from bottom.

BO 8(7,7)

10"(11",12") 52(56,62) STS

Work in ST ST.

#6

CO 52(56,62) STS. Work in K1,P1 rib.

#3

1"

10" (10½",11")

26" (28",30")

14" (15½",17")

1"

Sleeves

1. With #3 needles, cast on 56 (60, 64) sts. Work in K1, P1 rib for 1", following striping sequence #1.

2. Switch to #6 needles. Cont until work measures 13" from bottom.

3. Beg sleeve-cap shaping:
   - Bind off 6 (6, 7) sts at beg of next 4 rows.
   - Bind off 6 (7, 7) sts at beg of next 4 rows.
   - Bind off 7 (7, 7) sts at beg of next 4 rows.
   - Bind off last 20 sts.

Finishing

1. Sew shoulder seams.

2. Front bands: With RS facing and #3 circular needle, pick up a total of 291 (315, 339) sts, using the reverse striping sequence of bottom bands:
   - 128 (140, 152) sts from lower right front to shoulder seam
   - 35 sts from shoulder seam to shoulder seam
   - 128 (140, 152) sts from shoulder seam to lower left front
   - Work in K1, P1 rib for 5 rows. On buttonhole side, work 6 button-

   holes in 3rd row of ribbing, spacing them evenly between bottom and first neck decrease. Beg first buttonhole 3 sts from beg of row. Bind off.

3. Sew on buttons to correspond with buttonholes.

4. Sew in sleeve caps; sew side and sleeve seams.

5. Block assembled sweater to desired measurements.

6. Stabilize back neck and shoulders.

SLEEVE

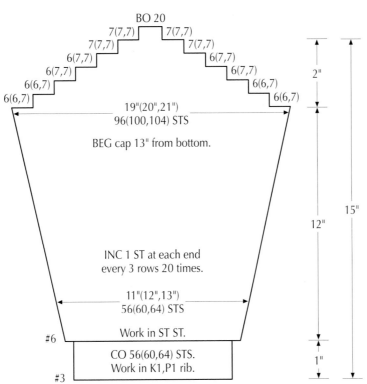

BO 20

7(7,7)   7(7,7)
7(7,7)   7(7,7)
6(7,7)   6(7,7)
6(7,7)   6(7,7)
6(6,7)   6(6,7)
6(6,7)   6(6,7)

19"(20",21")
96(100,104) STS

BEG cap 13" from bottom.

2"

INC 1 ST at each end every 3 rows 20 times.

15"

12"

11"(12",13")
56(60,64) STS

Work in ST ST.

#6

CO 56(60,64) STS.
Work in K1,P1 rib.

1"

#3

Collectible Cable

SHORT CABLED PULLOVER

As much as we like to believe that each sweater idea comes from some mysterious, creative well somewhere deep within us, in reality, most truly great sweaters we have created at Tricoter were inspired by something, or someone we saw.

This particular sweater was inspired by a much more pedestrian version in a well-known national catalog. We changed the dimensions and the neckline, but we loved the big chunky cables in the original sweater. Part of the art of great design is in the editing of the inspiration!

Size

Small (Medium, Large)
Finished Bust: 40" (44", 48")
Finished Length: 18" (20", 22")

Materials

*Use a bulky yarn that knits at 5.0 sts to
1" over cable pattern for the body
and 4.0 sts to 1" over rib pattern for
the sleeves.*

14, (15, 16) skeins of Trendsetter
Dolcino, each approximately
99 yds. [1400 (1500, 1600) yds. total]
#10 1/2 and #10 3/4 needles
#10 1/2 circular needle (20")
Cable needle
Stitch markers
Row counter
Stitch holder

*Note: Remember that when measuring
the width on a cable pattern, your work
will draw in considerably as you knit. To
get an accurate measurement, knit
halfway across the row, then, with the
yarn divided equally on the two needles,
spread the work as you would to steam.
This will give you a more accurate actual
width.*

Gauge

Front and Back: 20 sts and 24 rows
= 4" in cable pattern using #10 3/4
needles
Sleeves: 16 sts and 22 rows = 4" in rib
pattern using #10 3/4 needles
Always check gauge before starting
sweater. Increase or decrease
needle size to obtain correct gauge.

*Note: To determine gauge, cast on 19 sts
using the 2 sts on each end as purl sts
(RS) and the center 15 sts as your cable
(see cable pattern stitch below.)*

Rib Pattern Stitch

Row 1 (WS): *K2, P3, rep from *,
end K2.
On remaining rows, work stitches as
they face you, remembering to knit
the edge stitches (page 133).

Cable Pattern Stitch

Row 1: Small (RS): K4, *P3, K15, P3,
K4, rep from * 4 times.
Medium (RS): K1, P2, K4, *P3, K15,
P3, K4, rep from * 4 times,
end P2, K1.

Large (RS): K1, P8, K4, *P3, K15, P3,
K4, rep from * 4 times, end P8, K1.
Row 2, 4, 6, 8: Work stitches as they
face you.
Row 3: Work across to first K15.
- ◆ Put next 5 sts on cable needle
  and hold to back of work.
- ◆ Knit next 5 sts from left-hand
  needle.
- ◆ Knit 5 sts off of cable needle.
- ◆ Knit next 5 sts.
- ◆ Work across row to next K15 and
  repeat as above. Repeat across
  row.
Row 5 & 7: Repeat row 1.
Row 9: Work sts as they face you to
first 15-st cable, then:
- ◆ Knit next 5 sts.
- ◆ Put center 5 sts on cable needle
  and hold to front of work.
- ◆ Knit next 5 sts.
- ◆ Knit 5 sts off of cable needle.
- ◆ Work across row to 15-st cable
  and repeat as above. Repeat
  across row.
Row 10: Repeat row 2.
  Repeat rows 1–10.

Back

1. With #10½ needles, cast on 97 (102, 112) sts. Work in rib pattern stitch for 1½".
   - Inc 7 (8, 10) sts evenly across last row of ribbing.
2. Switch to #10¾ needles. Work in cable pattern stitch. Place stitch markers on each side of K15 to indicate cable position.
3. At 8" (9½", 10½") from bottom, beg armhole shaping:
   - Bind off 2 (4, 5) sts at outside edge at beg of next 2 rows, then:
     Small: Dec 1 st at beg of next 4 rows.
     Medium: Dec 1 st at beg of next 6 rows.
     Large: Bind off 4 sts at beg of next 2 rows; dec 1 st at beg of next 8 rows.

   All sizes should have 96 sts on the needle and measure 19" wide.
4. Cont until work measures 16½" (18½", 20½") from bottom.
5. Beg back neck and shoulder shaping:
   - Bind off first 7 sts. Work next 21 sts. Keeping 22 sts on right-hand needle, bind off center 38 sts. Finish row. Turn work.
   - Bind off first 7 sts. Finish row. Turn work.
   - Dec 1 st at neck edge. Finish row. Turn work.
   - Bind off 7 sts. Finish row. Turn work.
   - Work across row. Turn work.
   - Bind off 7 sts. Finish row. Turn work.
   - Work across row. Turn work.
   - Bind off last 7 sts.
6. Complete back neck and shoulder shaping:
   - Join yarn at neck edge. Dec 1 st and finish row. Turn work.
   - Bind off 7 sts. Finish row. Turn work.
   - Work across row. Turn work.
   - Bind off 7 sts. Finish row. Turn work.
   - Work across row. Turn work.
   - Bind off last 7 sts.

BACK

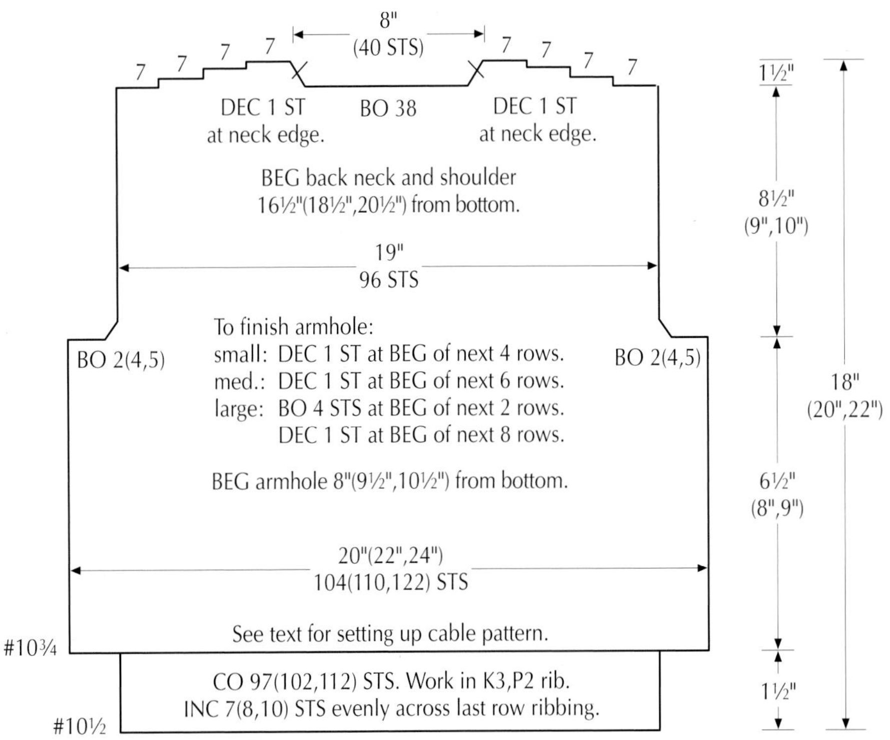
8"
(40 STS)
7 7 7 7
7 7 7 7
DEC 1 ST
at neck edge.
BO 38
DEC 1 ST
at neck edge.
BEG back neck and shoulder
16½"(18½",20½") from bottom.
19"
96 STS
To finish armhole:
small: DEC 1 ST at BEG of next 4 rows.
med.: DEC 1 ST at BEG of next 6 rows.
large: BO 4 STS at BEG of next 2 rows.
DEC 1 ST at BEG of next 8 rows.
BO 2(4,5)
BO 2(4,5)
BEG armhole 8"(9½",10½") from bottom.
20"(22",24")
104(110,122) STS
See text for setting up cable pattern.
#10¾
CO 97(102,112) STS. Work in K3,P2 rib.
INC 7(8,10) STS evenly across last row ribbing.
#10½
1½"
8½"
(9",10")
6½"
(8",9")
1½"
18"
(20",22")

Front

1. Work the front exactly the same as the back until work measures 15" (17", 19") from bottom.

2. Beg front neck shaping:
   - ◆ Work first 43 sts. Put center 10 sts on a stitch holder. Finish row. Turn work.
   - ◆ Work across row. Turn work.
   - ◆ Bind off 5 sts at neck edge. Finish row. Turn work.
   - ◆ Work across row. Turn work.
   - ◆ Bind off 3 sts at neck edge. Finish row. Turn work.
   - ◆ Work across row. Turn work.
   - ◆ Bind off 2 sts at neck edge. Finish row. Turn work.
   - ◆ Work across row. Turn work.
   - ◆ Bind off 2 sts at neck edge. Finish row. Turn work.
   - ◆ Work across row. Turn work.
   - ◆ Dec 1 st at neck edge EOR 3 times.

3. Cont until work measures 16½" (18½", 20½") from bottom.

4. Beg shoulder shaping:
   - ◆ Bind off first 7 sts at outside edge. Finish row. Turn work.
   - ◆ Dec 1 st. Finish row. Turn work.
   - ◆ Bind off 7 sts at outside edge. Finish row. Turn work.
   - ◆ Dec 1 st. Finish row. Turn work.
   - ◆ Bind off 7 sts at outside edge. Finish row. Turn work.
   - ◆ Dec 1 st. Finish row. Turn work.
   - ◆ Bind off last 7 sts.

5. Complete second half of front neck and shoulder shaping the same as first, but reverse the shaping.

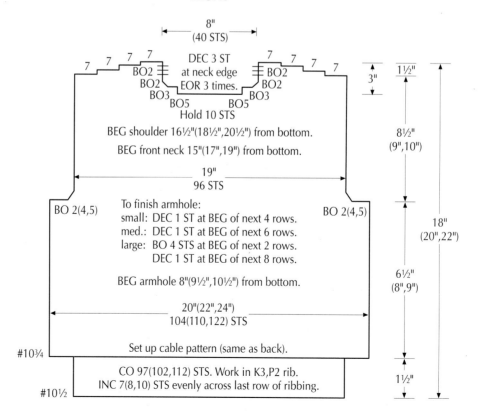

FRONT

8"
(40 STS)

7 7 7 7 DEC 3 ST at neck edge EOR 3 times. 7 7 7

BO2 BO2 BO2 BO2
BO3 BO5   BO5 BO3
Hold 10 STS

3"   1½"

BEG shoulder 16½"(18½",20½") from bottom.

BEG front neck 15"(17",19") from bottom.

8½"
(9",10")

19"
96 STS

BO 2(4,5)   BO 2(4,5)

To finish armhole:
small: DEC 1 ST at BEG of next 4 rows.
med.:   DEC 1 ST at BEG of next 6 rows.
large: BO 4 STS at BEG of next 2 rows.
        DEC 1 ST at BEG of next 8 rows.

BEG armhole 8"(9½",10½") from bottom.

18"
(20",22")

6½"
(8",9")

20"(22",24")
104(110,122) STS

Set up cable pattern (same as back).

#10¾

CO 97(102,112) STS. Work in K3,P2 rib.
INC 7(8,10) STS evenly across last row of ribbing.

1½"

#10½

Sleeve Pattern Stitch

Multiple of 4, plus 2 edge stitches:

Row 1 (WS): K1, *K3, P1, rep from *, end K1.

On remaining rows, work stitches as they face you, remembering to knit the edge stitches (page 133).

Sleeves

1. With #10³/₄ needles, cast on 34 (36, 36) sts. Work in pattern stitch for 2" [8¹/₂" (9", 9") wide].

2. Work sleeve increases:
   - ◆ Inc 1 st at each end every 4 rows 14 (15, 17) times in pattern.

3. Cont in pattern stitch until work measures 14" (15", 16") from bottom [62 (66, 70) sts; 15¹/₂" (16¹/₂", 17¹/₂") wide].

4. Work sleeve-cap shaping:
   - ◆ Bind off 2 (4, 5) sts at beg of next 2 rows.
   - ◆ Bind off 3 sts at beg of next 14 rows.
   - ◆ Bind off last 16 (16, 18) sts.

Finishing

1. Sew shoulder seams.

2. Neckband: With RS facing and #10¹/₂ circular needle, pick up a total of 80 sts:

- ◆ 45 sts across front from shoulder to shoulder
- ◆ 35 sts from shoulder to shoulder across back neck
- ◆ Work in K3, P2 rib for 3". Bind off in pattern.

3. Sew in sleeve caps; sew side and sleeve seams.

4. Block assembled sweater to desired measurements.

5. Stabilize back neck and shoulders.

SLEEVE

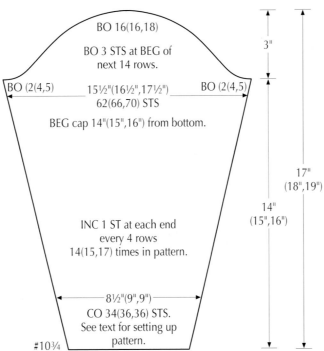

BO 16(16,18)

BO 3 STS at BEG of next 14 rows.

BO (2,4,5)   15¹/₂"(16¹/₂",17¹/₂")   BO (2,4,5)
62(66,70) STS

BEG cap 14"(15",16") from bottom.

3"

INC 1 ST at each end every 4 rows 14(15,17) times in pattern.

17" (18",19")

14" (15",16")

8¹/₂"(9",9")
CO 34(36,36) STS.
See text for setting up pattern.

#10³/₄

Some Knitting

Basics

There are a few knitting basics that may be second nature to many knitters, but we have found they can never be repeated too many times. Here is our list of basics.

Casting On

Cast on to a needle one size larger than the one specified, then change to the specified needle size on your first row. This ensures that your cast-on row is not too tight.

Knitting Your Edges Stitches

We always knit the first and last stitch of every row (including purl and pattern rows). This creates a clean, uniform "selvage edge" for weaving pieces together when the garment is complete.

Picking Up Dropped Stitches

It is not unusual to drop a stitch and for that stitch to ravel down one or more rows. A crochet hook is very helpful in picking up dropped stitches. Simply insert the hook, front to back, into the loop of the dropped stitch. Use

the hook to catch the first horizontal "ladder" in the knitting and pull it through the loop to the front. Continue in this manner through all the ladders. Place the loop on the needle, making certain that the right side of the U is on the front of the needle.

If you drop a stitch on a purl row, simply turn the work around and correct as described above for the knit side, making sure to turn the work back around to finish the purl row. Or, you can pick up the dropped stitch from behind by inserting the crochet hook, back to front, into the loop of the dropped stitch, placing the first horizontal ladder in front of the stitch and pulling the ladder through the loop to the back. Continue in this manner through all the ladders. Place the last loop on the needle, making sure the right side of the U is on the front of the needle.

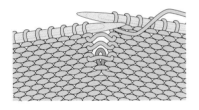

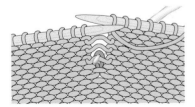

Picking up a dropped purl stitch

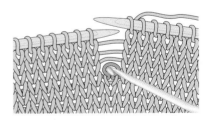

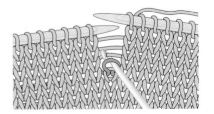

Picking up a dropped knit stitch

When an edge stitch drops and ravels, there will be no visible ladders to chain up with a crochet hook. Instead, you will see a large loop extending from the edge above a small loop, below which the knitted edge is intact. To

Facing page: a collection of beautiful Missoni yarns from Italy

correct this error, insert the crochet hook into the small loop. Holding the large loop with some tension, pull the lower portion of the large loop through the loop on the hook to form a stitch; then pull the upper part of the large loop through the loop on the hook to form a stitch; finally, catch the working yarn and pull it through the loop on the hook. Place the last stitch on the needle.

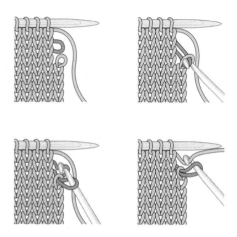

Picking up a dropped edge stitch

Joining Yarns

There are several methods of joining yarns when starting a new skein or changing colors. We like to knit both the old and new yarn into the first stitch as you begin a row, then, dropping the old yarn, continue across the row. Remember when you work back across the row, that first stitch is just one stitch, even though you have two strands in the stitch.

Start a new skein of yarn at the beginning of a row whenever possible. When changing in the middle of a row cannot be avoided, DO NOT knot the yarn. Leave a generous 3" tail from both the old and new skeins and continue knitting. These ends can be woven in securely and invisibly—knotting your yarns will leave a "scar" in your work.

Weaving in Ends As You Knit

To avoid hours of laborious darning after your sweater is complete (particularly on sweaters where you change yarns frequently, or in two-color work), you should get into the practice of weaving in the ends as you go.

It is important that the weaving is done at a relaxed, even tension, or the knitting will pucker. To do this, leave ends of approximately 3" on the old and new yarns; work the next two stitches with the new yarn, then, holding both yarns in your left hand, lay them over the working yarn and work the next stitch. Continue in this way, laying the ends over the working yarn on every other stitch and knitting past the ends on the following stitch for at least 2".

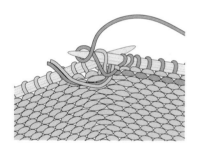

Increasing Your Stitches

There is more than one way to increase the number of stitches on your needle. You can make two stitches out of one by knitting into the front and back of the same stitch. This may also be done purlwise, by purling into the front and back of the same stitch, or it may be worked by knit 1, purl 1 into one stitch, or by purl 1, knit 1 into one stitch.

Another method, called "Make One," adds a new stitch without leaving a hole. Insert the left-hand needle from front to back into the horizontal strand between the last stitch worked and the next stitch on the left-hand needle. Knit this strand through the back loop to twist the stitch.

Decreasing Your Stitches

There are also several ways to decrease the number of stitches on your needle. With the yarn in back, slip one stitch, knit one stitch, and pass the slipped stitch over; that is, insert the point of the left-hand needle into the slipped stitch and draw it over the knit stitch and off the right-hand needle.

You can also slip the first and second stitches knitwise, one at a time, then insert the tip of the left-hand needle into the fronts of these two stitches from the left, and knit them together from this position. This is known as slip, slip, knit.

For V-neck ribbing with one center stitch, slip two as to knit, knit one; pass the slipped stitch over. For V-neck ribbing with two center stitches, knit two together and then slip, slip, knit.

Knitting Basic Cables

For a front cross, leave the cable needle holding the stitch(es) in front of the work while working the other stitches behind it.

For a back cross, leave the cable needle holding the stitch(es) in back of the work while working the other stitches in front.

For a twisted rib, knit the second stitch first in back of the work without taking it off the needle, then knit the first stitch as usual. Take both stitches off the left-hand needle.

Binding Off

Binding off secures the last row of knitting so that it will not ravel. Binding off is also used for shaping when two or more stitches need to be eliminated at one time, such as at armholes or necklines.

Always bind off in pattern. Many knitters tend to bind off too tightly, causing puckers and undue stress on the bound-off edge. You can prevent this problem by binding off with a knitting needle one or two sizes larger than the one called for in the pattern.

To bind off on a knit row, first knit two stitches, then * with the two stitches on the right-hand needle, pass the right stitch over the left and off the end of the needle. Knit the next stitch. Repeat from * until the required number of stitches are bound off.

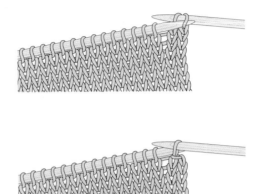

The process is the same for binding off on the purl side, except that you'll purl instead of knit. For ribbing, or for any other pattern stitch, bind off in the pattern; that is, knit the knit stitches and purl the purl stitches, always passing the right stitch over the left and off the end of the needle. If you bind off all the stitches on the needle, cut the working yarn and pull the cut end through the last stitch to secure it.

Finishing

Finishing is the art that separates homemade from handmade sweaters. There are many ways to execute most finishing techniques. We have included specific methods that we find work best for the sweaters in this book. When you have finished all the pieces of your garment, lay them out and measure them against the pattern for each piece again. It is much easier to make any corrections or alterations at this point, rather than waiting until the garment is sewn together. Pin the pieces together and try the garment on before burying the ends or sewing the pieces together.

Sewing Shoulder Seams

This method seams the shoulders by pulling the seaming yarn tight enough to cover the bound-off edges. The finished seam resembles a knit row. This seam requires the same number of stitches on each bound-off edge.

Working from the right side with the bound-off edges lined up stitch for stitch, begin by inserting a threaded tapestry needle from back to front into the V of the stitch just below the bound-off edge. *Insert the needle under two strands of the knit stitch on the opposite piece, then under the next two strands of the first piece. Adjust the tension so that the seam looks like the knitted work; repeat from * to the end of the bound-off edge.

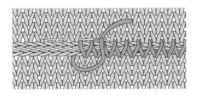

Sewing Side Seams

Work this seam from the right side of the knitting, placing the pieces to be seamed on a table, right side up. Begin at the lower edge and work upward, row by row. Insert a threaded tapestry needle under two horizontal bars between the first and second stitches from the edge on one side of the seam, then under two corresponding bars on the opposite side. Continue taking stitches alternately from side to side. Pull the yarn in the direction of the seam, not toward your body, to prevent the bars from stretching to the front.

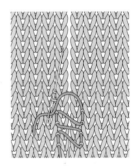

Picking Up Stitches to Knit Bands

Stitches are picked up to create finished neckbands, cardigan borders, and collars. Always pick up stitches from the right side, using a separate skein of yarn and a needle one or two sizes smaller than you used to knit the body of the garment.

For neckbands, begin at the right corner of the edge where you are picking up stitches. Insert the needle under two strands of the selvage-edge stitch, wrap the needle as if to knit, pull the loop through to the right side, and leave the newly made stitch on the needle. Continue working from right to left. Picked-up stitches can cause holes to form in the garment, especially along curved edges. Watch for these and, if you see one, take out that stitch and pick it up elsewhere. Continue until the desired number of stitches are on the needle.

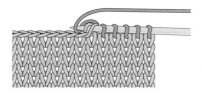

When picking up stitches along the vertical front edge of a cardigan, you will be picking up from the side, not the top of the stitch. The formula for picking up the correct number of evenly spaced stitches is as follows: Your edge stitches form a series of small "bumps" or points along the selvage edge. Beginning at the right side of the work, insert the needle into the hole under the first bump. Now insert your needle into the hole underneath the bar between the first two bumps; repeat in the bar between the second and third bumps. Pick up the fourth stitch in the hole behind the third bump. Repeat this process (bar, bar, bump) along the vertical length of the front band.

To make sure the picked-up stitches are evenly spaced, divide the knitted edge into fourths (or eighths for a very long edge) and mark these divisions with open stitch markers. Pick up one-fourth (or eighth) of the desired total number of stitches in each section.

Many patterns will tell you to "pick up and knit" a specific number of stitches. Read literally, this is somewhat misleading—you should not pick up a stitch and then knit it. You should pick up a stitch as if to knit it, then leave it on the needle. When all the stitches are on the needle, turn the work and begin your pattern in the next row.

Setting in Sleeve Caps

With the right side of the pieces facing you, fold the sleeve in half lengthwise to find the center. Pin the center point of the cap to the outer edge of the shoulder seam, then

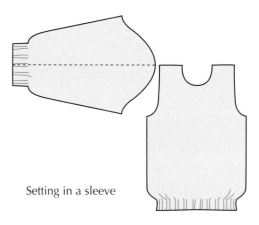

Setting in a sleeve

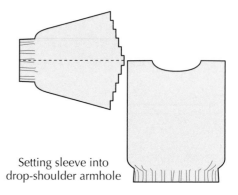

Setting sleeve into drop-shoulder armhole

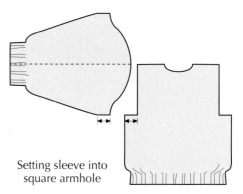

Setting sleeve into square armhole

pin the beginning point of the sleeve-cap shaping to the lowest point of the armhole, both front and back. Now ease the cap into the armhole evenly and pin in place. Sew in the sleeve as you would a side seam, taking care not to pull the working yarn too tight so it does not distort the armhole.

Note that we do some cap shaping even with drop-shoulder patterns; this eliminates the bulk of extra fabric under the arms when the sweater is sewn together. To set in a drop shoulder where there is no armhole shaping on the body of the sweater, measure from the shoulder seam to the desired armhole depth and place pins both front and back to identify the sleeve placement.

When setting a sleeve into a square armhole, fit the sides of the sleeve directly into the body of the sweater at the bound-off armhole stitches, then ease in the cap from the shoulder seam in each direction.

Buttonholes

A visible horizontal buttonhole is neat, firm, and requires no reinforcing. The lower edge of the buttonhole is worked from the right side of the garment, and the upper edge is worked from the wrong side.

To work a one-row buttonhole:

1. Work to the position where you want the buttonhole, bring the yarn to the front, slip the next stitch purlwise, and then return the yarn to the back.

2. * Slip the next stitch; then on the right-hand needle, pass the second stitch over the end stitch and drop it off the needle. Repeat from * 3 times. Slip the last bound-off stitch to the left needle and turn the work.

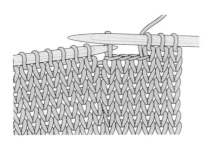

3. Move the yarn to the back and use the cable cast-on to cast on 5 stitches as follows: * Insert the right needle between the first and second stitches on the left needle, draw up a loop, and place it on the left needle. Repeat from * 4 times. Turn the work.

4. With the yarn in back, slip the first stitch from the left needle and pass the extra cast-on stitch over it to close the buttonhole. Work to the end of the row.

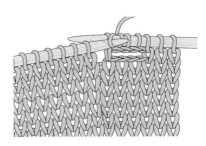

To correctly space buttonholes, one buttonhole needs to be within a couple of stitches from the top of the band, and one a couple of stitches from the bottom. The balance of the buttonholes should be evenly spaced between the top and bottom holes. (Exceptions may occur when the front bands, neck, and/or collar are to be crocheted rather than knit.) Select your buttons before knitting the buttonholes rather than trying to find a button that fits the hole.

Crocheted Edges

Crocheted edges are usually narrower than knitted borders and provide a simple, clean edge. Single crochet and reverse crochet (also called shrimp or crab stitch) are the most popular crocheted edges for knitted garments. Single crochet makes a smooth finish; crab stitch makes a decorative beadlike finish.

Single Crochet

Working from right to left, insert the crochet hook into the knit edge stitch, draw up a loop, bring the yarn over the hook, and draw this loop through the first one. * Insert the hook into the next stitch, draw up the loop, bring the yarn over the hook again, and draw this loop through both loops on the hook; repeat from * until the entire edge has been covered. Cut the yarn and secure the last loop by pulling the tail through it.

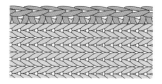

Crab Stitch (reverse crochet or shrimp stitch)

We always work one row of single crochet first, then follow with a row of crab stitch. Working from left to right, insert the crochet hook into a single crochet stitch, draw up a loop, bring the yarn over the hook, and draw this loop through the first one. * Insert the hook into the next stitch to the right, draw up a loop, bring the yarn over the hook again, and draw this loop through both loops on the hook;

repeat from * until the entire edge has been covered. Cut the yarn and secure the last loop by pulling the tail through it.

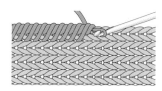

Stabilizing Back Neck and Shoulders

We stabilize all our sweaters to anchor the seams and to keep them from growing or stretching across the shoulders, causing them to appear sloppy or ill fitting.

Work one row of chain stitch on the inside shoulder seam of the sweater from one shoulder across the back neck to the opposite shoulder. If necessary, pull in slightly by increasing the tension as you work to narrow the shoulders and neck up to an inch on each side as needed for proper fit.

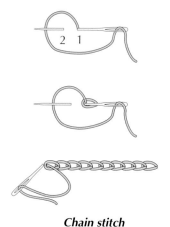

Chain stitch

Blocking

Blocking is the process of dampening or steaming the knitted pieces to even out the lines of the stitches and the yarn fibers. For best results, block the pieces before you sew them together. The labels on most knitting fibers give instructions for blocking. Read the instructions before you begin.

Blocking requires a flat surface larger than the largest knitted piece. Block on an out-of-the-way place on the carpet or make a special padded "steaming table" for this purpose: Layer particle or peg board with heavy batting (or $1/4$"- to $1/2$"-thick foam) and a sturdy fabric, such as canvas duck. Wrap the surface fabric to the back, and use a staple gun to attach it to the wood. We covered our steam table at the shop with a plaid sheet. The plaid's grid is helpful in lining up edges.

Use long straight pins, such as quilting or T-pins, to pin the pieces to the blocking surface. First pin the length of the piece, then the width, and finally the curves and/or corners, measuring carefully at every step to ensure that it matches the dimensions given in the pattern. Place pins every 1" to prevent the piece from shrinking as it dries. If you block on a very large surface, such as a carpet, you may pin the pieces next to each other, lining up the selvage edges that will be steamed to make sure the seams are even.

Hold a steamer or iron set on the steam setting $1/2$" above the knitted surface and direct the steam over the entire surface, except the ribbing. There are several good hand steamers on the market today in the \$40 to \$50 range. You can get similar results by placing wet cheesecloth on top of the knitted surface and touching it lightly with a dry iron. Do not press down or use a forward or sideways motion.

Never steam-block ribbing that you want to remain elastic, such as in the waist and cuff area. Once blocked, ribbing will remain stretched out. However, you should block ribbing along a front cardigan border to flatten it and prevent it from pulling.

Press the seams of your garment as they are sewn. Take care not to mash the yarn in the seam area, but do dampen the seam on the inside of the garment, using steam or a spray bottle (according to yarn type) and gently finger-press the seam to reduce the bulk. This also serves to set the seaming yarn and prevents the yarn ends from working their way out.

Hand-knit garments can be machine washed on the gentle cycle in your washing machine in a sweater (net) bag. Washing with a very mild soap (we recommend Forever New) and drying flat on a drying rack will ensure long life. Remove as much water as possible by running the sweater through the washer's spin cycle or pressing it between dry towels before laying it flat to dry. Make sure the water temperature on both wash and rinse cycles is cool.

RESOURCES

Tricoter Services

It is our commitment at Tricoter to offer the most luxurious, unique fibers and ornamentation available in the European and domestic markets and to assist you in the design and creation of your own one-of-a-kind, hand-knit garment or home accessory. Tricoter offers complimentary design services and guidance through the completion of projects to all of our customers. We believe that it is the detail and finishing that elevates a garment from "loving-hands-at-home" to a beautiful hand-knit original. Therefore, we offer a variety of classes from basic skills through advanced techniques and finishing.

Because we realize your time is precious, Tricoter is also pleased to offer a variety of custom knitting and finishing services for those occasions when you require

professional assistance. We have a number of out-of-town customers with whom we work on a regular basis to assist in the completion of hand-knit garments. The following is a brief outline of our services:

♦ Expert finishing services are available at an hourly rate. You can turn your work-in-progress over to us at any stage.
♦ We offer a variety of custom knitting services for your convenience. All garments are individually fitted and beautifully finished. We will work with you to design and create a sweater, jacket, coat, or garment of your choice that reflects your individual style.
♦ We have one of the most extensive collections of the finest hand-painted needlepoint canvases, fibers, and accessories available in the Pacific Northwest. We offer both individual and small-class instruction for needle-work, and professional blocking and finishing for all of your needlepoint projects.

We have an appreciation for beautiful fibers and fine design, and we share our expertise and assistance with you—from the selection of fibers to a design that reflects your individual style. Please feel free to contact us for additional information regarding any of these services.

Tricoter

3121 E. Madison Street
Seattle, WA 98112
Phone: (206) 328-6505
Fax: (206) 328-0635
Toll Free: 1-877-554-YARN
         1-877-554-9276
E-mail: tricoter@aol.com
Web Site: www.tricoter.com

Yarn Resources

Filatura di Crosa, Missoni & The Stacy Charles Collection
    S. Charles Collezione Yarns:
    1059 Manhattan Avenue
    Brooklyn, NY 11222
    (800) 962-8002
Prism Yarns:
    Prism
    2595 30th Avenue North
    St. Petersburg, FL 33713
    (813) 327-3100
Noro & Schachenmayr Yarns:
    Knitting Fever, Inc.
    35 Debevoise Avenue
    Roosevelt, NY 11575-0502
    (800) 645-3457
Adrienne Vittadini Yarns:
    JCA, Inc.
    35 Scales Lane
    Townsend, MA 01469-6340
    (800) 225-6340
Colinette Yarns:
    Unique Kolours, Ltd.
    1428 Oak Lane
    Downington, PA 19335
    (800) 252-3934

Lang Yarns:
    Berroco, Inc.
    14 Elmdale Road
    Uxbridge, MA 01569-0367
    (800) 343-4948
Trendsetter Yarns:
    Trendsetter
    16742 Stagg Street, Unit 104
    Van Nuys, CA 91406
    (800) 446-2425

BIBLIOGRAPHY

Fassett, Kaffe. *Glorious Knits.* New York: Clarkson N. Potter, Inc., 1985.

Complete Guide to Needlepoint. Pleasantville, N.Y.: Reader's Digest Association, Inc., 1979.

Square, Vicki. *The Knitter's Companion.* Loveland, Colo.: Interweave Press, Inc., 1996. The best "carry-along" reference book we've found. Small, sturdy, lightweight, and very complete!

Vogue Knitting. New York: Pantheon Books, 1989. The comprehensive source to your hand-knitting questions in easy-to-understand language with clear, concise illustrations.

Books from Martingale & Company

Martingale
& COMPANY

That Patchwork Place   FIBER STUDIO PRESS   Pastimes

Crafts

15 Beads: A Guide to Creating One-of-a-Kind Beads
The Art of Handmade Paper and Collage
Making Memories with Fabric, Photos,
   and Family Keepsakes
Christmas Ribbonry
Folded Fabric Fun
Hand-Stitched Samplers from I Done My Best
The Home Decorator's Stamping Book
A Passion for Ribbonry
Welcome Home: Debbie Mumm

Home Decorating

Decorate with Quilts & Collections
The Home Decorator's Stamping Book
Living with Little Quilts
Make Room for Quilts
Soft Furnishings for Your Home
Welcome Home: Debbie Mumm

Needle Arts/Ribbonry

Christmas Ribbonry
Crazy Rags
Hand-Stitched Samplers from I Done My Best
Miniature Baltimore Album Quilts
A Passion for Ribbonry
A Silk-Ribbon Album
Victorian Elegance

Surface Design/Fabric Manipulation

15 Beads: A Guide to Creating One-of-a-Kind Beads
The Art of Handmade Paper and Collage
Complex Cloth: A Comprehensive Guide
   to Surface Design
Dyes & Paints: A Hands-On Guide to
   Coloring Fabric
Hand-Dyed Fabric Made Easy

Wearables

Crazy Rags
Dress Daze
Dressed by the Best
Easy Reversible Vests
More Jazz from Judy Murrah
Quick-Sew Fleece
Sew a Work of Art Inside and Out
Variations in Chenille

Quilts

Appliqué

Appliquilt® Your ABCs
Baltimore Bouquets
Basic Quiltmaking Techniques for Hand Appliqué
Coxcomb Quilt
The Easy Art of Appliqué
Folk Art Animals
From a Quilter's Garden
Stars in the Garden
Sunbonnet Sue All Through the Year
Traditional Blocks Meet Appliqué

Borders and Bindings

Borders by Design
The Border Workbook
A Fine Finish
Happy Endings
Interlacing Borders
Traditional Quilts with Painless Borders

Design Reference

All New! Copy Art for Quilters
Blockbender Quilts
Color: The Quilter's Guide

Design Essentials: The Quilter's Guide
Design Your Own Quilts
Freedom in Design
The Log Cabin Design Workbook
The Nature of Design
QuiltSkills
Sensational Settings
Surprising Designs from Traditional Quilt Blocks

Foundation/Paper Piecing

Classic Quilts with Precise Foundation Piecing
Crazy but Pieceable
Easy Machine Paper Piecing
Easy Mix & Match Machine Paper Piecing
Easy Paper-Pieced Keepsake Quilts
Easy Paper-Pieced Miniatures
Easy Reversible Vests
Go Wild with Quilts
Go Wild with Quilts—Again!
A Quilter's Ark
Show Me How to Paper Piece

Hand and Machine Quilting/Stitching

Loving Stitches
Machine Needlelace and Other Embellishment
   Techniques
Machine Quilting Made Easy
Machine Quilting with Decorative Threads
Quilting Design Sourcebook
Quilting Makes the Quilt
Thread Magic
Threadplay with Libby Lehman
Stripples
Stripples Strikes Again!
Strips That Sizzle
Two-Color Quilts

Miniature/Small Quilts

Beyond Charm Quilts
Celebrate! with Little Quilts
Easy Paper-Pieced Miniatures
Fun with Miniature Log Cabin Blocks
Little Quilts All Through the House
Lively Little Logs
Living with Little Quilts
Miniature Baltimore Album Quilts
No Big Deal
A Silk-Ribbon Album
Small Talk

Quiltmaking Basics

Basic Quiltmaking Techniques for Hand Appliqué
Basic Quiltmaking Techniques for Strip Piecing
A Perfect Match
Press for Success
The Ultimate Book of Quilt Labels
Your First Quilt Book (or it should be!)
Hand-Dyed Fabric Made Easy

Rotary Cutting/Speed Piecing

Around the Block with Judy Hopkins
All-Star Sampler
Bargello Quilts
Block by Block
Down the Rotary Road with Judy Hopkins
Easy Star Sampler
The Joy of Quilting
Magic Base Blocks for Unlimited Quilt Designs
A New Slant on Bargello Quilts
Quilting Up a Storm
Rotary Riot
Rotary Roundup

Simply Scrappy Quilts
Square Dance
Stripples
Stripples Strikes Again!
Strips That Sizzle
Two-Color Quilts

Seasonal Quilts

Appliquilt® for Christmas
Easy Seasonal Wall Quilts
Folded Fabric Fun
Quilted for Christmas
Quilted for Christmas, Book II
Quilted for Christmas, Book III
Quilted for Christmas, Book IV
Welcome to the North Pole

Theme Quilts

The Cat's Meow
Celebrating the Quilt
Class-Act Quilts
The Heirloom Quilt
Honoring the Seasons
Kids Can Quilt
Life in the Country with Country Threads
Making Memories with Fabric, Photos,
   and Family Keepsakes
More Quilts for Baby
Once Upon a Quilt
Patchwork Pantry
Quick-Sew Celebrations
Quilted Landscapes
Quilted Legends of the West
Quilts: An American Legacy
Quilts for Baby
Quilts from Nature
Through the Window and Beyond

Watercolor Quilts

Awash with Colour
More Strip-Pieced Watercolor Magic
Strip-Pieced Watercolor Magic
Watercolor Impressions
Watercolor Quilts

Many of these books are available through
your local quilt, fabric, craft-supply, or art-
supply store. For more information, call, write,
fax, or e-mail for our free full-color catalog.

Martingale & Company
PO Box 118
Bothell, WA 98041-0118 USA

1-800-426-3126
International: 1-425-483-3313
24-Hour Fax: 1-425-486-7596
Web site: www.patchwork.com
E-mail: info@martingale-pub.com

11/98